# QUR'ANIC PICTURES OF THE UNIVERSE

## The Scriptural Foundation of Islamic Cosmology

# QUR'ANIC PICTURES OF THE UNIVERSE

## The Scriptural Foundation of Islamic Cosmology

OSMAN BAKAR

UBD PRESS

IBT

*Jointly published by*

UBD PRESS
Universiti Brunei Darussalam,
Jalan Tungku Link,
Gadong BE 1410,
Brunei Darussalam.

Islamic Book Trust
607 Mutiara Majestic
Jalan Othman
46000 Petaling Jaya
Selangor, Malaysia
*www.ibtbooks.com*

Islamic Book Trust is affiliated with The Other Press.

ISBN: 978-967-0526-26-3 (hardcover)
ISBN: 978-967-0526-25-6 (pbk.)

*Printed in Malaysia*

# Contents

# Acknowledgements

I wish to record my thanks to the Royal Aal al-Bayt Institute for Islamic Thought in Amman, the Hashemite Kingdom of Jordan for its generous research grant that enabled me to undertake a major research on a scientific exegesis (*tafsīr ʿilmī*) of the Qur'an. I reserved my special thanks in particular for its Chairman of the Board of Trustees, His Royal Highness Prince Dr Ghazi bin Muhammad bin Talal, an internationally renowned royal patron of learning and scholarship and interfaith dialogue and intellectual-activist in contemporary Islam. The content of this book, now published for the first time, forms part of a much larger work that was envisaged in the original research plan covered by the grant and that is yet to be completed. I also wish to express my thanks to UBD PRESS of Universiti Brunei Darussalam for kindly agreeing to publish this book in collaboration with the Kuala Lumpur-based Islamic Book Trust (IBT) and The Other Press. The staff of IBT, especially Tuan Hj Koya Kutty and Encik Yusoff Sultan, deserve special praise for their invaluable contribution to the book's publication. Last, but not least, are my thanks to the staff and students of Sultan Omar ʿAli Saifuddien Centre for Islamic Studies (SOASCIS), Universiti Brunei Darussalam and my grown up children both for their roles as critical commentators, the former at my place of work and the latter at home.

Osman Bakar, PhD
No. 2, The Core, Universiti Brunei Darussalam
Jalan Tungku Link, Gadong, BE1410, Brunei Darussalam

18 Jumādā'l-ākhir 1437
27 March 2016

# Introduction

بسم الله الرحمن الرحيم

*In the Name of God, the Most Gracious, the Most Merciful*

This book is about the multiple visions of the cosmos or the Universe as perceived through the lens of the Qur'an that claims for itself a unique distinction as the last sacred scripture to be divinely revealed to mankind. Although the Qur'an's visions of the Universe are many and varied, indeed infinite in number as will be shown later, this book only seeks to discuss a limited number of them that may be viewed as among the easiest to understand. To be precise, altogether five visions of the Universe are discussed in the book. Each vision of the Universe produces what we refer to as its corresponding picture. Accordingly, we have chosen *Qur'anic Pictures of the Universe* as the main title of this book. Each vision or picture is shaped by a set of verses gathered from various chapters of the Qur'an that appear to us as displaying conceptual coherence and thematic unity not only among themselves but also with other pictures of the Universe.

The five cosmic pictures discussed in this book depict the Universe in five corresponding ways. The first picture (Chapter Three), which we call the *astronomical*, depicts the Universe as a vast celestial space-time complex that is constituted of such cosmic entities as planetary and stellar systems, galaxies and constellations governed by laws. The second picture (Chapter Four), which we describe as the *architectural*, depicts the Universe as an architectural work that is divinely planned, designed and constructed. Viewed as a whole, the Universe is seen through this picture as an edifice with a solid construction, a perfect architectural design, and beautiful ornamentation. The third picture (Chapter Five) depicts the Universe as *a divine kingdom* that extends from the Divine Throne (*al-'arsh*) to the furthest region of the material world where the planet Earth, the home of God's vicegerents (sing: *khalīfah*), namely the human species, is situated. An integral component of this picture is the cosmic web of causal relations governed by God's laws that exist between the different parts and forces of the Universe. The fourth picture (Chapter Six) depicts the Universe as a system of layers of light and darkness. Through this picture we are able to see the creatures populating the Universe being positioned in a hierarchical order according to degrees of light that are present in them. The fifth and final picture, which is discussed in details in Chapter Seven and which we call the *microcosmic*, appears as the most unique of them all. It depicts man as a perfect replica of the whole Universe. Thus it may be viewed as a picture of the Universe that contains all of its other pictures.

Chapter Two of this book provides a brief explanation of the fundamental reason why there is necessarily an infinite number of pictures of the Universe. The fundamental reason in question is metaphysical or theological in nature. According to the Qur'an, the Divine Names and Qualities are manifested in the whole of creation. In other words, the Universe as a whole may be viewed as God's Self-Disclosure (GSD), meaning Disclosure of His Names and Qualities. Since God's Names and Qualities are infinitely many, as particularly emphasized by such Sufi theologians as al-Ghazzālī (1058-1111) and Ibn al-'Arabī (1165-1240), the GSD Principle means that the images of the Universe are likewise necessarily infinite in number. We have found Ibn al-'Arabī's exposition of the GSD Principle that he treated as his key cosmological doctrine to be extremely useful to our study of selected Qur'anic pictures of the Universe in this book and in the larger work of which it is a part, which is yet to be completed. Other Qur'anic pictures of the Universe that are treated in the rest of our work in a coming publication include images of the Earth as the sole human planetary home and of the Universe variously pictured as a mathematical book, a living system or as the "Big Man" (*al-insān al-kabīr*), a cosmic balance (*mīzān*), a world of intelligences, a quantum world, and a directory of signposts for man's spiritual journey to beyond the Universe.

In studying Qur'anic pictures of the Universe, this book may be viewed as a work on scientific exegesis (*tafsīr 'ilmī*) of the Qur'an. In actual fact, the research project for which we received a generous grant from the Royal Aal al-Bayt Institute for Islamic Thought in Amman, the Hashemite Kingdom of Jordan and of which this book is its initial output pertains wholly to the subject of scientific exegesis of the Qur'an. However, in our approach to this genre of exegetical work we chose to adopt a thematic treatment of the relevant verses of the Qur'an. It seems quite clear to us that the Qur'an features the Universe and its numerous pictures and images as one of its most attractive and interesting themes for human reflection and contemplation and scientific study. To our satisfaction we find that a thematic exegesis of a selected set of Qur'anic verses that is associated with a particular picture of the universe promises a better knowledge outcome for us both in terms of its depth and breadth than does a piecemeal exegesis of one or two so-called cosmic or creation verses (*al-āyāt al-kawniyyah*) that is usually motivated by the reductionistic epistemology of modern science. Moreover, through such a thematic approach that is inspired instead by Islam's holistic (*tawḥīdic*) epistemology we are able to acquire a more coherent and unified view of the Universe. Our preferred methodological approach to scientific exegesis in a broader sense as adopted in this book is of the thematic and synthetic kind. In this kind of approach revealed metaphysical data and principles are synthetized with the empirically acquired scientific data in a harmonized fashion. Central to this approach is the epistemological role of the previously mentioned GSD Principle.

Viewed as a whole, we maintain that this book presents a new study of one of the major themes of the Qur'an. The theme of Qur'anic pictures of the universe treated here pertains to as yet still a little explored facet of Islamic cosmology. Through this particular thematic study of the Qur'an we argue that this book is able to offer some new insights into the subject of cosmology that will prove particularly helpful to those interested in deepening their understanding of Qur'anic perspectives on cosmology, the natural sciences, and religion and science. It is our sincere hope that through this book we will be able to make a humble contribution to a better contemporary understanding of the scriptural foundation of Islamic cosmology and its branches and the present discourse on epistemology of scientific exegesis (*tafsīr ʿilmī*) of the Qur'an. Befitting the contents of the book in which all the pictures of the Universe under study are totally based on revealed data in the Qur'an we choose the phrase "the scriptural foundation of Islamic cosmology" as its subtitle. *Wa bi'Llāh al-tawfīk wa'l-hidāyah wa bihī nastaʿīn.*

*Chapter One*

# Definitions of the Universe in the Qur'an

The Qur'an teaches the idea of a God-centric cosmos or universe[1] by which we mean it is defined in terms of God. It provides the basis for the definition of the universe that was to be universally accepted throughout the history of Islamic thought. According to this general definition, as provided by the Muslim thinkers, the universe is the sum total of "everything other than God" (*mā siwā Allāh*).[2] It is clear from this definition that the universe is conceived in terms of another reality that transcends and comprehends it, namely God. The Qur'an is interested in defining and clarifying the various kinds of relationships that exist between the universe and God. These relationships, which are all metaphysical in

1. In the English language, the words cosmos and universe are understood to have the same meaning, connoting the same ontological reality. However, for the sake of consistency, we are using the word universe throughout this work instead of the word cosmos.

2. For discussions of this definition of the universe, see Osman Bakar, 'Cosmology,' John Esposito, ed., *The Oxford Encyclopedia of the Modern Islamic World* (New York-Oxford: Oxford University Press, 1995), vol. 1, pp. 322-323; see also William C. Chittick, *The Self-Disclosure of God: Principles of Ibn al-'Arabī's Cosmology* (Albany: State University of New York Press, 1998), p. xvii-xviii.

nature, serve as the foundational elements of Islamic cosmology.[3]

Terminologically, several Arabic words that find usage in the Qur'an are used to denote the universe. These words are *al-'ālamīn* (singular: *'ālam*), *al-khalq*, and *al-kawn*. The plural word *al-'ālamīn*[4] occurs seventy-three times in the Qur'an, while the singular word *al-'ālam* does not occur even once.[5] However, as a scientific term to denote the universe as a single entity, the word *al-'ālam* in the singular is preferred, because it conveys in a clear manner the idea of the universe as a single whole that is viewed as other than God. Viewed from the scientific perspective, the many worlds (*al-'ālamīn*) of which the Qur'an speaks in numerous contexts constitute subsystems of this single universe.

The first time *al-'ālamīn* occurs is at the beginning of the Opening Chapter (*Sūrah al-Fātiḥah*): "Praise be to God, the Guardian-Lord and Sustainer of all the worlds (*rabb al-*

---

3. For an excellent exposition of the various metaphysical relationships between God and the universe as the foundational elements of Islamic cosmology, according to Ikhwān al-Ṣafā' (flourished: fourth century A.H./tenth century C.E.), Abū Raiḥān Muḥammad ibn Aḥmad al-Bīrūnī (362 A.H./973 C.E. – 421 A.H./1030 C.E., and Ibn Sīnā, see Seyyed Hossein Nasr, *An Introduction to Islamic Cosmological Doctrines* (Cambridge, USA: Harvard University Press, 1964); also (Boulder: Shambala, 1978) edition. For Ibn al-'Arabī's detailed discussion of the same theme, see William Chittick, *The Self-Disclosure of God.*

4. The word *al-'ālamīn* is the genitive case of the plural of *'ālam*, namely *al-'ālamūn* or *al-'awālim*, which does not appear in this noun form in the Qur'an.

5. See *corpus.quran.com/qurandictionary.jsp.*

*'ālamīn*)."[6] Its last occurrence is in Chapter 83 (*Sūrah al-Muṭaffifīn*): "A day when all mankind will stand before the Lord of the worlds (*rabb al-'ālamīn*)."[7] What a significant and beautiful occurrence and arrangement it was indeed for these two verses! The first occurrence of *rabb al-'ālamīn* is in connection with man's praise (*taḥmīd*) of God for bringing out into existence the whole universe, including the physical world where he is providentially placed. The verse in view does not explicitly mention where the human world is located. Neither do the rest of the verses in the Chapter mention it. However, in several other verses of the Qur'an the locus of the human world is identified with the planet Earth. In accordance with the Divine Cosmic Plan the Adamic or human species is given the Earth as their temporary planetary home. The Qur'an says: "We said: "Get you down, all [you people] with enmity between yourselves. On earth will be your dwelling place (*mustaqarr*) and your means of livelihood for a time.""[8] This verse appears to be telling human beings that the Earth is not only their temporary planetary home but also the only one that is suitable for human life.[9] Man's life on this temporary planetary home is

---

6. *The Qur'an*, chapter 1 ("The Opening"), verse 2.

7. *The Qur'an*, chapter 83 ("The Dealers in Fraud"), verse 6.

8. *The Qur'an*, chapter 2 ("The Cow"), verse 36.

9. We have argued in another article why the claim that the Earth is man's only planetary home possible despite the vastness of the Universe stands on solid ground. See Osman Bakar, "Understanding the Challenge of Global Warming in the Light of the Qur'an's idea of Earth as our only planetary home", Imtiyaz Yusuf (ed.), *A Planetary And Global Ethics For Climate Change And Sustainable Energy*, (Bangkok: Konrad-Adenauer-Stiftung, and Mahidol University, 2016).

what we call his terrestrial life. It is a life that is to be dedicated to the service and worship of God. In other words, it is about man's journey from God to his temporary home on the planet Earth. The last occurrence of *rabb al-'ālamīn*, however, is about man's return journey to God and his meeting with Him on the Great Assembly Day for all mankind. Forty-two times (57.5%) the word *al-'ālamīn* occurs as part of the phrase *rabb al-'ālamīn*, which since the early history of Islam easily passes as one of the most popular spiritual formulae uttered by Muslim tongues.

The word *khalq* has a number of meanings. Its predominant meaning, however, is creation. It is mentioned fifty-two times in the Qur'an, but out of this total number of occurrences, it is only in twenty-seven cases[10] that it conveys the meaning of the whole creation, which is to be identified with the cosmos. Further, in eight out of the twenty-seven cases in which *al-khalq* denotes the cosmos, the word occurs together with *samāwāt* ("heavens") and *arḍ* ("earth") in the single phrase *khalq al-samāwāt wa'l-arḍ* ("creation of the heavens and the earth"). The first such occurrence is in the following verse:

> Verily in the creation of the heavens and the earth (*khalq al-samāwāt al-arḍ*); in the alternation of the night and the day; in the sailing of the ships through the ocean for the profit of mankind; in the rain which Allah sends down from the skies, and the life which He gives therewith to an earth that is dead; in the beasts of all kinds that He scatters through the earth; in the change of the winds, and the clouds which they trail like their slaves between the sky and the earth – (here) indeed are

10. For this numerical data, see *corpus.quran.com/qurandictionary.jsp.*

signs (*āyāt*) for a people that are wise (*qawm ya'qilūn*).[11]

The last occurrence of *khalq al-samāwāt wa'l-arḍ* is in this verse: "And among His signs is the creation of the heavens and the earth, and the living creatures that He has scattered through them; and He has power to gather them together when He wills."[12] Here again, we may wish to take note of a significant feature pertaining to the first and last occurrences of the phrase *khalq al-samāwāt wa'l-arḍ*. In the first occurrence, the emphasis is on signs of God as displayed in creation as a source of spiritual knowledge and wisdom for man in fulfillment of the ultimate purpose of his existence. In the last occurrence, the emphasis is on the return of God's signs, that is, the creatures, to Him and hence on the temporal limitation imposed on the duration of these signs for man's spiritual benefits. However, the last verse in which the word *khalq* appears with the meaning of the whole created order and thus the whole cosmos is in a later chapter: "He Who created the seven heavens one above another: no want of proportion will you see in the creation of the Most Gracious (*khalq al-Raḥmān*). So turn your vision again: do you see any flaw? (*fuṭūr*)."[13]

From the perspectives of our present work on scientific exegesis, this verse is illustrative in a good number of ways. First, the Divine Name *al-Raḥmān*, which is one of the sixteen fundamental ideas in the Opening Chapter, is repeated here in connection with the creation of the seven heavens. The Names

---

11. *The Qur'an*, chapter 2 ("The Cow"), verse 164.

12. *The Qur'an*, chapter 42 ("Consultation"), verse 29.

13. *The Qur'an*, chapter 67 ("The Dominion"), verse 3.

*al-Raḥmān* ("The Absolute Good and the Most Gracious") and *al-Raḥīm* ("The Most Merciful"), which appear together in the Opening Chapter, refer to the twin faces of Divine Mercy (*Raḥmah*).[14] *Al-Raḥmān* refers to creative mercy, and *al-Raḥīm* to saving mercy. The Divine Attribute and Quality of *Al-Raḥmān* manifests itself in creation with all of its creaturely content. God as *al-Raḥmān* created all creatures out of His Infinite Mercy regardless of whether or not they prove the worthiness of their creation.

In the Opening Chapter, the Name *al-Raḥmān* occurs in relation to the cosmos (*al-'ālamīn*) as the manifestation of His creative Mercy (1:2). The Name is repeated 56 times in other parts of the Qur'an. In conformity with the theory of the *mathanian* character of the Qur'an[15], the Name *al-Raḥmān* appears in the verse just quoted (67:3) in relation to the creation of the seven heavens. The verse describes beautifully the seven heavens as *khalq al-Raḥmān* ("the creation of the Most Gracious") and explains in further details the verse 1:2 in the Opening Chapter. It describes the heavens as flawless and a perfect work of creation, and thus illustrates one of the manifestations of God's creative Mercy. Significantly, in this verse man is invited to verify for himself God's claim about the flawlessness in the heavens He has created. The second time He

---

14. On the fine distinction between the meanings of *al-Raḥmān* and *al-Raḥīm*, see al-Ghazzālī, *The Ninety-Nine Beautiful Names of God*, pp.52-57.

15 We derive the word *mathanian* from the Qur'anic term *mathani*, which conveys the idea of repetition of a doctrine or statement of truth in manifold forms. See *The Qur'an*, chapter 39 ('The Throngs') verse 23. In our view, the theory of the *Mathanian* character of the Qur'an is contained in this verse.

invites man to verify it, He says, "Do you see any flaw?" What a beautiful invitation to men of science to study and reflect on God's creation so as to verify His claims!

The verse 67:3 may also be cited to illustrate the existence and significance of the various cosmic pictures displayed in the Qur'an. One of these pictures is what we call the "architectural picture," which is to be discussed in Chapter Four of this book, since it refers to the universe viewed as a work of architecture that displays perfect and beautiful design and construction. The verse would also be extremely relevant to a discussion on the theme of the planet Earth as man's only home. We will discuss there the function of the heavens as the perfect roofs of our planetary home.

For the purpose of showing that the words *al-khalq* and *al-'ālamīn* are both used to signify the universe the following verse is instructive, not to mention its significance in several other ways:

> Your Guardian-Lord (*Rabbukum*) is God, Who created the heavens and the earth (*al-samāwāt wa'l-arḍ*) in six days, and is firmly established on the Throne [of authority]: He draws the night as a veil over the day, each seeking the other in rapid succession; He created the sun, the moon, and the stars, [all] governed by laws under His command. Do not creation (*al-khalq*) and its affairs belong to Him? Blessed be God, the Cherisher and Sustainer of the worlds (*al-'ālamīn*)![16]

Our immediate interest in this verse pertains to the issue of the universe being signified by both the terms *al-khalq* and *al-'ālamīn*. It is quite clear from the composition of the verse that

16. *The Qur'an*, chapter 7 ("The Heights"), verse 54.

*al-samāwāt wa'l-arḍ*, *al-khalq*, and *al-'ālamīn* all refer to the same entity, namely the universe as a whole. We may infer from this fact that the universe consists of the heavens and the earth. More precisely, on the basis of verse 67:3 earlier cited and many similar references to the seven heavens, the universe consists of seven heavens and the earth. The above verse further informs us that the sun, the moon, and the stars are part of the heavens.

Additionally, the above verse is significant to our discussion of the Qur'anic pictures of the universe. This time, the picture most visible projected by the verse is what we call the "astronomical picture," although there may be one or two other pictures that may be developed out of this verse. It is quite clear from the verse that astronomical phenomena feature the most prominently as indicated by the phenomenon of night and day seeking each other in rapid succession and the astronomical laws governing the movement and behavior of the sun, the moon, and the stars. It seems that the verse is also emitting a mathematical picture of the cosmos as indicated by the reference to the creation of the heavens and the earth in six days and as implied by the reference to the sun, the moon, and the stars as being governed by God's laws, which science informs us are essentially mathematical in nature.

The third term used to signify the cosmos is *al-kawn*. The noun *al-kawn* is derived from the root verb *kāna*, which conveys among others the meanings of to be and to exist. Thus, from this root word we also have the noun *kā'in*, meaning "being" and "existent." The noun *al-kawn*, which is used widely to signify the world, the cosmos, being, and existence, is not found in the Qur'an. But its verb form appears 1358 times in this Sacred Text. This quantity includes the 8 times the word *kun* ("Be!") appears in the Book to signify the Divine Command.[17] The noun *al-kawn* is sometimes used in the sense of being in reference to God such as we encounter in the phrase *al-kawn al-aʿlā* ("The Supreme Being"). The adjective *kawnī* is used to signify that which relates to the cosmos or the universe. In other words, it is to convey the meaning of "cosmic." Some contemporary Muslim religious scholars have used the phrase *al-āyāt al-kawniyyah* ("cosmic verses") in referring to the verses of the Qur'an pertaining to cosmic reality and phenomena. This term is therefore closely related to the notion of "scientific verses" that we discussed at length in our larger work on scientific exegesis of the Qur'an.

There is another observation to be made regarding words and phrases used by the Qur'an to signify the cosmos. Other than the words *al-ʿālamīn* and *al-khalq*, the Qur'an also uses the phrase *mā fī al-samāwāt wa mā fi'l-arḍ*,[18] meaning "all that is in the heavens and on earth," to denote the cosmos. The significant thing to be noted is that all these terms used to signify the cosmos have meanings that relate it to God. More specifically, they each have meanings that point in a clear manner to the specific metaphysical relationships between the cosmos and God. The beauty of the Arabic language is that,

17. The Qur'an says: "Be! And it is (*kun fayakūn*)." See the appearance of the phrase *kun fayakūn* in the following eight verses of the Qur'an: chapter 2 ("The Cow"), verse 117; chapter 3 ("The Family of ʿImrān"), verses 47 and 59; chapter 6 ("The Cattle"), verse 73; chapter 16 ("The Bee"), verse 40; chapter 19 ("Mary"), chapter 36 ("Yā Sīn"), verse 82; chapter 40 ("The Forgiver"), verse 68.

18. This phrase occurs many times in the Qur'an. It's first occurrence is in chapter 2 ("The Cow"), verse 284: "To God belongs all that is in the heavens and on earth."

through its unique "algebraic" root-word system, it is able to capture in the widest sense possible the semantic field of each word as well as to offer the clearest explanation possible of the relationship between a "name" and the corresponding "named."

The word *'ālam,* understood either as "world as a subsystem of the cosmos" or "cosmos as a single entity" is etymologically related to the word *'ilm* ("knowledge") and *'ālim* ("knower"). However, the relationship between knowledge (*'ilm*) or the possessor of knowledge (*'ālim*) and the world (*'ālam*) is not only etymological but also metaphysical. The world is named *'ālam* in Arabic, because it is meant to point to the knowledge (*'ilm*) and its possessor (*'ālim)* that originate or manifest it as a separate reality. According to classical Arabic lexicons, the word *'ālam* ("world") is "primarily a name for that by means of which one knows [a thing]."[19] In other words, *'ālam* is that by which the *'ilm* that originates it is known or identified. When this relationship between *'ālam* and *'ilm* or *'ālim* is now envisaged at the metaphysical-theological level as is done in the science of Qur'anic exegesis, the name *'ālam* takes the predominant meaning of "that by means of which the Creator is known."[20] More precisely, the name *'ālam* points to the reality that God as *al-'Alīm* ("The All-Knowing") is the metaphysical source of *al-'ālam.*

The metaphysical relation between the cosmos and God is not only envisaged as the relation between it as the object of knowledge (*'ālam* in the singular or *al-'ālamīn* in the plural) and God as the All-Knowing or Possessor of Knowledge (*al-*

---

19. See Edward William Lane, *Arabic-English Lexicon*, vol. 2, p. 2140.

20. Edward W. Lane, *Arabic-English Lexicon*, vol. 2, p. 2140.

*'Alīm*), but also in other forms of relationships. The key phrase *rabb al-'ālamīn* ("The Lord of all the worlds") itself expresses the metaphysical relation between the cosmos (*al-'ālamīn*) and God as *al-Rabb* ("The Cherisher and Sustainer"). Then, we have another metaphysical relation as implied by the word *khalq*. The noun *khalq* is derived from the root verb *khalaqa*, the active participle of which is *khāliq*. The root verb *khalaqa* conveys the primary idea of "measuring or determining the measure, proportion, or the like, of a thing; and the making a thing by measure, or according to the measure of another thing; or proportioning a thing to another thing."[21] In conformity with this primary meaning of *khalaqa*, the active participle *khāliq* has been used to refer to a leather worker, because it is his profession "to measure first and then cut."[22]

Yusuf 'Ali summarizes the meanings of *khalaqa* gathered by Lane by saying that this word involves "the idea of measuring, fitting it into a scheme of other things."[23] When the epithet *khāliq* is applied to God we have the following meaning: "[God as] *al-Khāliq* ... is He Who brings into existence according to the proper measure, or proportion, or adapation."[24] According to al-Ghazzālī, the core meaning of *khalaqa* is *taqdīr*, which means "determination of measurement" so that when this meaning is applied to God we have His Attribute and Quality, *al-Khāliq*, as meaning the Planner (*al-Muqaddir*).[25] Al-Ghazzālī

---

21. Edward W. Lane, *Arabic-English Lexicon*, vol. 1, p. 799.

22. Edward W. Lane, *Arabic-English Lexicon*, vol. 1, p. 802.

23. 'Abdullah Yusuf 'Ali, *The Meaning of the Holy Qur'an*, p. 47.

24. Edward W. Lane, *Arabic-English Lexicon*, vol. 1, p. 802.

25. Al-Ghazzālī, *The Ninety-Nine Beautiful Names of God*, p. 68.

asserts that "God is *khāliq* inasmuch as He is the Planner (*muqaddir*)." Regardless of what the precise meaning of *al-khāliq* is, in reference to God, our discussion of the etymological relation between *khalq* and *khāliq* leads us to the notion of a metaphysical relation between the cosmos as the domain of all creatures (*khalq*) and God as the Creator (*al-Khāliq*).[26] This particular metaphysical relation between the cosmos and God is best summarized by the phrase *khāliq al-khalq* ("the Creator of the world of creatures"). The important point to be observed is that, in using the word *khalq* to signify the cosmos, we will always be reminded by its meaning that the cosmos has a creator.

Similarly, the word *kawn* is etymologically related to verbs that are associated with Divine Activities in the cosmos. Quite well-known to the Muslims generally is the association of the verb "be!" with God's creative command *kun* that brings the cosmos (*kun fayakūn*) and its creaturely content into being. According to the Qur'an, the created order comes into existence through the divine creative command *kun* ("Be!").[27] For this reason, the term *kawn*, which conveys the meaning of engendered existence, is often used by Muslim cosmologists to refer to the whole cosmos. Consequently, one of the terms used to denote cosmology is *'ilm al-kawn*, meaning literally "the science of the cosmos." In this case again, the Muslim mind is constantly reminded that the cosmos viewed as *al-kawn* is metaphysically related to God's creative command in the eternal "now."

---

26. The Divine Name *al-Khāliq* is mentioned 12 times in the Qur'an.

27. We have referred earlier to all the eight verses of the Qur'an in which the Divine creative command *kun* is mentioned. See note 16.

In the light of our discussion of the meaning of the cosmos in the Qur'an and the various words used in it to signify the cosmic identity, we may assert that although the cosmos is defined as a reality other than God, their metaphysical relationship is always preserved. The traditional Muslim vision of the cosmos is not as an independent reality but as an entity that always depends on God for its existence. The Islamic cosmos is not self-generated and self-sustained as believed in modern cosmology. On the contrary, it is generated and sustained by a transcendent power, namely the Divine Reality.

The dominant metaphysical relationship between the cosmos and God in the Muslim mind, indeed in the Qur'an itself, is the causal relationship between creation and Creator that is best signified by the oft-repeated formula *rabb al-'ālamīn* and to a lesser extent by the phrase *khāliq al-khalq*. The idea of the cosmos as a "reality" that is dependent on God is also evident in all the other forms of their metaphysical relationship that have been contemplated by the Muslim minds. The idea of the cosmos as God's Self-Disclosure as expounded by Ibn al-'Arabī's school of Sufism provides perhaps the most direct relationship conceivable between the two in the sense that it almost removes away from the human mind the notion of the cosmos as a reality other than God. In a sense, the various pictures of the cosmos discussed in this chapter result from the various forms of relationship that exist between it and God.

The first Muslim to have defined the universe was Ibn 'Abbās. In his commentary (*tafsīr*) on the Qur'an, he gave a definition of the universe that was to be adopted by Muslims of the later generations. His definition was contained in his brief explanation of the term *al-'ālamīn* in the phrase *rabb al-*

*'ālamīn*, which forms part of the second verse of the opening chapter. He interprets *rabb al-'ālamīn* to mean "*rabb* of every living creature on the face of the earth and every inhabitant of the heavens (*ahl al-samā'*)."[28] He explains *rabb* as meaning "the Lord of the jinn and mankind (*sayyid al-jinn wa'l-ins*), the Creator of all creatures (*khāliq al-khalq*), their Nourisher and Sustainer (*razzāquhum*), and their Developer and Evolver from one state to another (*muḥawwiluhum min ḥal ilā ḥal*)."[29]

It may be inferred from Ibn 'Abbās' commentary on the phrase *rabb al-'ālamīn* that the word *al-'ālamīn* is to be understood as meaning the whole universe, since it comprises everything other than God. This universe comprises the earthly and the heavenly creatures, of which he specifically mentions only the jinn species and the human species as examples. In short, the phrase *rabb al-'ālamīn* describes the relationship between God as *rabb* and the cosmos (*al-'ālamīn*) as the world of His creatures. Ibn 'Abbās' coinage of the phrase *khāliq al-khalq* provides the earliest instance of the usage of the Qur'anic term *al-khalq*[30] to convey the meaning of the cosmos or the whole created order. As previously discussed, this term became accepted in Islamic cosmology as another Arabic word besides *al-'ālam* or *al-'ālamīn* to denote the cosmos.

Ibn 'Abbās has another important connection with Islamic cosmology. He transmitted the most detailed hadith on the

28. See *Tafsīr Ibn 'Abbās*, p. 2.

29. *Tafsīr Ibn 'Abbās*, p. 2.

30. The word *al-khalq* is found in many verses of the Qur'an. See, for examples, 2:164; 10:4; 36:78-79.

Prophet's night and ascension journey (*isrā'* and *mi'rāj*)[31] from the lowest end of the cosmos, meaning the Earth, to the highest and beyond to the Divine Throne. This hadith is of great significance to Islamic cosmology, since it makes references to cosmological ideas and symbols.

If we examine the Muslim definitions of the cosmos in the later periods, we will find that they are merely detailed variants of Ibn 'Abbās' definition. One of these definitions was given by the Ikhwān al-Ṣafā' ("Brothers of Purity"), a group of scientists who flourished in the fourth century AH/tenth century CE and who created a detailed cosmology on the basis of the Qur'an. According to them, the cosmos comprises "all the spiritual and material beings who populate the immensity of the heavens, who constitute the reign of multiplicity which extends to the spheres, the stars, the elements, their products and to man."[32] It is clear that by inserting the terms "spiritual and material beings" in their definition and also mentioning their fundamental constituents, the Ikhwān further clarified the meaning of "all the worlds" and "everything in the heavens and the earth and what is in between" stated in Ibn 'Abbās' definition. The insertion of the terms in question itself has a basis in the Qur'an.[33]

---

31. For a discussion of Ibn 'Abbās' narrative on the night of ascension (*laylat al-mi'rāj*), see Abū 'Abd al-Raḥman al-Sulāmī, *The Subtleties of the Ascension: Early Mystical Sayings on Muhammad's Heavenly Journey* (Louisville, Kentucky: Fons Vitae, 2006), pp. 8-11.

32. *Rasā'il*; see also Seyyed Hossein Nasr, *An Introduction to Islamic Cosmological Doctrines.*

33. *The Qur'an,* Chapter 32 ('The Prostration'), verse 4.

*Chapter Two*

# Why There Are Many Pictures of the Universe in the Qur'an

The significance of the Qur'an for Islamic cosmology goes far beyond providing the basis of definition and terminologies to be adopted in referring to the cosmos. The Qur'an also provides numerous pictures of the cosmos that served as the basis for its scientific study by Muslims in the past. That there are many pictures of the cosmos to be found in the Qur'an is evident upon examination of its verses that deal with cosmic reality and phenomena. By a picture of the cosmos we mean one or more aspects of it that God has revealed for human visualization with specific purposes in mind. Each picture is viewed as having both scientific and spiritual meanings. The spiritual meaning it seeks to convey to the human mind pertains to the particular Divine Names and Qualities that are manifested in the cosmic phenomena in question. In its totality, the cosmos has been described by Sufi cosmologists as God's Self-Disclosure, meaning disclosure of His Names and Qualities.[34]

The different pictures of the cosmos reveal its many and

34. For a detailed discussion of the Sufi understanding of the cosmos as God's self-disclosure, see William Chittick, *The Self-Disclosure of God.*

diverse aspects as seen from various human positions befitting its ontological status as the world of multiplicity. The cosmos may be divided into its components in many different ways, depending on the bases or criteria of division to be adopted. In this chapter, we will present and discuss the most visible of these pictures as indicated by the cosmological data in the Qur'an itself. These cosmic pictures may also be seen as the most significant to science, not only for their past impact on Islamic science but also for their relevance to modern and contemporary cosmology and the various sciences that are its branches. However, before proceeding to discuss these cosmic pictures, it is perhaps pertinent to briefly address the issue of the significance of these multiple Qur'anic pictures of the cosmos for Islamic cosmology.

In our view, there have to be many pictures of the cosmos even within the same revelation, since from the human point of view, it would be impossible to perceive the whole of the cosmos with just "one look," "one picture," or "one image." The Islamic view of *imago Dei* ("God's image") necessitates not one but many *imago mundis* ("image of the world"). The significance of this truth for cosmology is that, while there is but one Islamic metaphysics based on oneness of the Divine Principle of *tawḥīd*, there are different cosmological schemes all of which are authentically Islamic. From the point of view of the microcosm, the human mind has been structured by God to know the whole of reality through multiple visions and levels of consciousness. In terms of multiplicity, this microcosmic fact would correspond in a one-to-one fashion to the macrocosmic reality. Thus, a human perception or visualization of the cosmos is always from a particular angle or perspective, but a single perception cannot comprehend the whole of the cosmos.

Although the Divine vision of the cosmic reality is one, when expressed in human language that vision has to be presented in multiple forms. For this reason, to the extent that a particular scientific theory of the cosmos represents a particular vision of it - but never the total vision of it - there had to be many cosmologies formulated and cultivated in one Islamic intellectual tradition. In Islamic civilization, we can observe several well-known cosmologies existing side by side. Each cosmology is based on a particular vision of the cosmos presented in the Qur'an. On the basis and within the framework of each cosmology, we have a particular group of scientists, philosophers or theologians who try to produce a science of the natural world.

**The many worlds as subsystems of the cosmos**

Although the cosmos consists of many kinds of worlds, it is one in the sense that it may be viewed as a single entity and a unified whole, characterized by order, balance, and harmony. We have referred earlier in this chapter to the word *al-ʿālam* in the singular as signifying the cosmos viewed as a single whole. It was, in fact, viewed as a single entity by some past Muslim thinkers and scholars, as can be inferred from the terminologies they used to denote it. For example, Jaʿfar al-Ṣādiq used the word *al-ʿālam al-kabīr* ("macrocosm") to denote the cosmos external to man and the word *al-ʿālam al-ṣaghīr* ("microcosm") to denote man as a being with a unique constitution as "an epitome of all that is in the big cosmos."[35] The Ikhwān al-Ṣafā' referred to the macrocosm as "the big

35. E. W. Lane, *Arabic-English Lexicon*, vol. 2, p. 2141.

man" (*al-insān al-kabīr*) with a body and soul.[36] They called the soul of the cosmos "the Universal Soul" (*al-nafs al-kullīyah*).

The cosmos is a unity in multiplicity and diversity. The unity of the cosmos is a reflection or manifestation of Divine Unity on the plane of relativity and creation. As the Qur'an asserts, "If there were in the heavens and the earth other gods besides God, there would have been confusion in both!"[37]It is God the One Who is the source of this unity in multiplicity. He created the cosmos so that the whole or every world (*'ālam*) that is a component of it would serve as a means by which He is known as the Creator. According to some commentators of the Qur'an, as highlighted by the classical lexicologists, the primary meaning of the Arabic word *al-'ālam* is "that by means of which the Creator is known."[38] It is extremely significant that in Islamic cosmology the purpose of the cosmos is even embedded in the etymological meaning of the very word used to denote it.

Arabic lexicology provides references to many kinds of *'ālam* (worlds) that find usage in the various sciences. Examples are the angelic world (*'ālam al-malā'ikah*),[39] the

36. See Seyyed Hossein Nasr, *An Introduction to Islamic Cosmological Doctrines*, p. 67.

37. *The Qur'an*, Chapter 21 ("The Prophets"), verse 22.

38. E. W. Lane, *Arabic-English Lexicon*, vol. 2, p. 2140.

39. All the angels taken together constitute a distinct world (*'ālam*). The angels are mentioned as a whole species in many verses, for examples, chapter 2 ("The Cow"), verse 30, which refers to God addressing all the angels on the cosmic occasion of the creation of Ādam as His *khalīfah* ("vicegerent") on the earth; chapter 2, verse 177 pertaining to man's obligatory belief in the whole angelic species; chapter 13 ("The Thunder"),

world of the jinn (*'ālam al-jinn*), the world of mankind (*'ālam al-ins*), the animal world (*'ālam al-ḥayawān*), the plant world (*'ālam al-nabāt*), and the mineral world (*'ālam al-ma'ādin*). Angels, jinn, and mankind, which were created in that order, are each mentioned in the Qur'an as a distinct species but without being referred to as *'ālam* ("world").[40] In the case of the animal, plant, and mineral worlds, the Qur'an does not refer to their existence as distinct species or worlds, but merely mentions examples of their respective members. Nonetheless, worth mentioning is that, terminologically speaking, while the word *al-'ālam* was used in classical Arabic to denote both the cosmos as a whole and each particular world of the species of which it is a part, the Qur'an uses only the plural word *al-'ālamīn* ("the worlds") to denote the whole cosmos.

The cosmos can be divided into its parts or components in various ways, because we may use different criteria or bases of division. Its division into the angelic world, the subtle world, and the physical world is perhaps the most fundamental of them. This is because this division is made on the basis of the fundamental nature of each of the three worlds. The angelic world is completely spiritual and is therefore beyond the perception of man's physical senses. It is created from spiritual

---

verse 13 pertaining to all the angels praising God; chapter 35 ("The Originator of Creation"), verse 1 pertaining to the nature and function of the angels as divine messengers. For more detailed discussion of the angelic world and its varied cosmic functions, see Sachiko Murata & William C. Chittick, *The Vision of Islam* (New York: Paragon House, 1994).

40. The Arabic word for angel is *malak*, but the Qur'an uses it mostly in the plural, *malā'ika* (88 times). The word *jinn* appears 22 times in the Qur'an. There is even a chapter of the Book titled "The *Jinn*." See chapter 72.

light (*nūr*), which itself admits of degrees of quality. The Qur'an teaches that the angels have cosmic functions pertaining to the worlds studied by science, particularly the world of life forms on the planet Earth. Likewise, the subtle world, which includes the jinn, has cosmic relations with the physical world in which man lives. Islamic science includes the study of these relations as an integral part of its scientific and epistemological concerns. As mentioned in the last chapter, jinn is made of "fire of a scorching wind,"[41] which is non-physical but a grosser form of light.

The physical world, which coincides with the physical cosmos and extends from the planet Earth to the furthest regions in the physical heavens, is perceptible to man's physical senses. The planet Earth is unique, since it home to many life forms, including man. According to traditional Islamic science, earthly creatures are made of the four elements of earth, water, fire, and air to varying degrees of perfection in their qualitative mixtures that make each life form unique. And man is a unique creature, since although an earthly creature he is an essential summary of all the worlds ("microcosm"). There is even something "divine" in man by virtue of the fact that God has breathed into Ādam of His Spirit (*min rūḥī*),[42]meaning that into man generally since Ādam symbolizes the human species.

---

41. *The Qur'an*, chapter 15 ("The Rocky Tracts"), verse 27.

42. *The Qur'an*, chapter 15 ("The Rocky Tracts"), verse 29: "When I have fashioned him [in due proportion] and breathed into him of My spirit, fall you down in obeisance unto him." See also chapter 38 ("Ṣād"), verse 72. Ādam is not mentioned by name in these verses, but is implied by the textual context in each case.

*Chapter Three*

# The Astronomical Picture of the Universe

In describing the various pictures of the cosmos as found in the Qur'an, our focus is on the physical cosmos. The first picture, which has been a popular one, depicts the observable cosmos as a planetary and stellar system and it may be termed an astronomical picture of the cosmos. It depicts the configuration of the celestial bodies focusing on those in our solar system, which have the greatest impact on the Earth, and describes their respective motions and configurations in space and their "function."

In classical Islamic science, astronomy was generally defined as the science of celestial bodies that deals mainly with their mathematical properties, which explains its treatment as one of the mathematical sciences. A concise definition of astronomy is provided by NASA: "Astronomy is the study of stars, planets, and space." Although issues of celestial physics feature prominently in modern astronomy – hence its inclusion among the physical rather the mathematical sciences – the core content of scientific knowledge in the discipline is still mathematical in nature. Literally, astronomy means the study of the stars (*'ilm al-nujūm*). However, even in Islamic science, the domain of astronomy is broader than simply the concern with the study of the stars. Nonetheless, the study of the stars remains a core element of astronomy, mainly because as self-luminous bodies with attractive properties, the stars present to the human eye with one of the most fascinating phenomena in the physical heavens. Since the cosmic picture at which we are looking now is about the stars, the planets, and space, naming it "the astronomical picture" seems quite appropriate.

The full astronomical picture depicts the cosmos, first of all, as a vast ocean of physical space in which are found a great multitude of celestial bodies displaying their respective positions, properties and qualities, and behaviors. We may call this physical space the cosmic space. According to the Qur'an, the cosmic space is expanding. In other words, this space is not static, or a constant thing. Rather, it is "dynamic," not contracting but extending and expanding. The Qur'an says: "With power and skill We constructed the firmament (*al-samā'*); truly, it is We who are steadily expanding it (*innā la-mūsi'ūn*)."[43] Modern science concurs with this interpretation of the verse that maintains the cosmic space is expanding, but scientists differ among themselves over the underlying cause of the expansion.

The interpretation of the verse we have given[44] is fully

43. *The Qur'an*, chapter 51 ("The Winds that Scatter"), verse 47.

44. Many modern exegetes or translators of the Qur'an, scientists, and religious scholars share the above interpretation of the verse. Yusuf 'Ali and Muhammad Asad agree with this view. See 'Abdullah Yusuf 'Ali, *The Meaning of the Holy Qur'an*, p. 1139; Muhammad Asad, *The Meaning of the Qur'an*, p. 964. Maurice Bucaille, a French medical scientist who is said to have converted to Islam, and quite well-known in the Islamic world for his attempt to reconcile Qur'anic scientific verses with modern science, also adopts the same interpretation of the verse. See his *The Bible, The Qur'an, and Science* (Indianapolis: North American Trust Publications, 1978), p.

justified on the basis of linguistic analysis, and we have argued in our larger work that in Islam, the linguistic method is a legitimate exegetical method. The plural verbal-noun *mūsi'ūn* (sing: *mūsi'*) is the active participle of the root verb of the fourth form (*awsa'a*), which conveys the meaning of "to extend and expand." So the phrase *innā la-mūsi'ūn* means "truly we are the expanders of it" or "we are expanding it." Quite clearly, in the context of the verse, the thing that is expanded refers to *al-samā'*, translated above as "the firmament." However, this firmament that is in a state of steady expansion and skillfully constructed by God needs to be further explained and identified, since by itself the verse cannot help us to conclusively show that it is the whole cosmic space that is expanding.

In the verse, the noun *al-samā'* occurs in the singular form, not in the plural. This textual fact raises the question of whether *al-samā'* here signifies only one firmament or all existing firmaments. The word *samā'* occurs in the Qur'an 310 times both in its singular and plural forms. The plural form, *samāwāt*, is used in some verses to simply mean all the existing heavens without mentioning their number, and in some others, to convey the message that the whole firmament comprises seven heavens. As an example, a previously cited verse says: "He [*i.e.* God] Who created the seven heavens above one

---

167. This popular book has seen many imprints and translations into various languages of the world, particularly the Muslim languages. For further references to exegetical works that lend support to the above interpretation, see The Supreme Council for Islamic Affairs, ed., *Al-Muntakhab fī tafsīr al-Qur'ān al-Karīm* ("Selections of Exegeses of the Holy Qur'an")(Cairo, 1973).

another ..."[45] It is important to be noted that the number seven is to be understood here not in the quantitative but rather qualitative sense. In traditional Islamic mathematics, the number seven is a symbol of perfection, notwithstanding the fact that in Arabic usage it is also synonymous with "several."

Unlike in modern mathematics, where numbers are viewed purely as quantities on which we can perform the arithmetical operations of addition and subtraction, and multiplication and division, in traditional Islamic mathematics numbers are understood as both quantities and qualities. We cannot perform such arithmetical operations on numbers as qualities. It is in this context of the theory of numbers that we need to understand the idea of numbers as symbols. The number seven symbolizes the quality of perfection. This symbolic meaning of number seven has a basis in the Qur'an, for the above restated portion of the verse 67:3 is immediately followed by this "challenge" from God to man to verify for himself whether he could find any flaw in His creation of the heavens: "no want of proportion will you see in the creation of [God] Most Gracious. So turn your vision again: do you see any flaw?" On the basis of this whole verse then, the seven heavens are equated with perfection in God's creation.

We therefore maintain that the phrases "all the heavens and the earth" and "the seven heavens and the earth" both refer to the whole cosmos. As for the verses in which the word *samā'* occurs in the singular form, it would be sufficient for us to cite one or two of them that have the word clearly signifying the seven heavens. It is evident that in some of these verses, its specific signification is to the visible sky, the region where we

---

45. *The Qur'an*, chapter 67 ("The Dominion"), verse 3.

could observe weather conditions and other meteorological phenomena such as cloud formations and movements, lightning, thunder, rains, and storms. In classical Islamic science, the visible sky is identified with the lowest *samā'*, which it calls the "*sublunary region*," that is, the sphere below the moon. In its first occurrence in the Qur'an, the word *samā'* conveys precisely this meaning. The verse reads: "Or [another similitude] is that of a rain-laden cloud from the sky (*al-samā'*): in it are zones of darkness, and thunder and lightning."46

Its second occurrence is in this verse: "Who has made the Earth your couch and the firmament (*al-samā'*) your canopy; and sent down rain from the sky (*al-samā'*)."[47] Twice in this verse the word *al-samā'* occurs in the singular form. Quite clearly here, *al-samā'* from which rain is sent down is identical to the *samā'* in the first occurrence. However, we do not think that *samā'* as man's canopy should be wholly identified with *samā'* as the source of rain. In our understanding, the word *samā'* in the former case refers to all the firmaments or heavens, although it occurs in the singular form. This *samā'* would be the all-embracing firmament of which the visible sky is its closest part to the Earth. One good argument in support of this interpretation is the cosmic dimension and significance of the functions of the Earth as couch and of the firmament as canopy as indicated in the "second occurrence" verse (2:22). The basis of this argument is provided by the following verse: "It is He Who has created for you all things that are on earth; moreover, His design comprehended the firmament (*al-samā'*), for He gave order and perfection to the seven heavens (*al-*

46. *The Qur'an*, chapter 2 ("The Cow"), verse 19.

47. *The Qur'an*, chapter 2 ("The Cow"), verse 22.

*samāwāt*); and of all things He has perfect knowledge."[48] Interestingly, this is the third occurrence of the word *samā'* in the singular, but this time it occurs together with its plural in conjunction with the number seven.[49] This verse is a key to the understanding of many other verses concerning the cosmic relations between the Earth and the heavens.

This verse clearly shows that *al-samā'* in its singular form is used in the Qur'an to refer to the firmament in its totality (*al-samā'*), which it equates with the seven heavens (*sab' samāwāt*) that have been given order and perfection (*sawwāhun*). We also observe that this usage of *al-samā'* to mean the seven heavens has a specific context, which we may define as a cosmological context in which the whole cosmos is kept in view and the planet Earth is sought to be compared and contrasted with the rest of the cosmos, that is, the seven heavens, in respect of their cosmic functions.[50] On the textual basis of the "third occurrence" verse, we may therefore deduce from it the important principle that whenever in a verse the word *samā'* in the singular is used in such a cosmological context, explicitly stated or otherwise, it is possible to interpret the word to mean the whole firmament comprising the seven heavens.

---

48. *The Qur'an*, chapter 2 ("The Cow"), verse 29.

49. We say "interestingly," because while the second occurrence of *samā'* in the singular points to the strong possibility of it referring to the seven heavens, its third occurrence confirms its usage as a plural.

50. The preceding verse (2:28) about man's cosmic journey to God and the succeeding verses (2:30-39) about the creation of Ādam and the cosmic role of the angels and the divine choice of the planet Earth as man's temporary home (2:36) demonstrate in a clear manner that, content-wise, the verse 2:29 has the whole cosmos in view.

Additionally, we may affirm the possibility of such an interpretation on a linguistic basis. Many classical lexicologists maintain that in the Arabic language *samā'* is used both as a singular and as a plural, depending on the context of its usage. Abū'l-Qāsim al-Rāghib al-Iṣfahānī (d. 502 A.H./1108 or 1109 C.E.), a well-known lexicologist and Qur'anic exegete, for example, says that "the *samā'* as opposed to the Earth (*al-arḍ*) is feminine and sometimes masculine, and is used as a singular and as a plural."[51] He maintains that the Qur'an itself adopts this mixed usage of the word *samā'*. To illustrate this point, he mentions verse 2:29, namely the "third occurrence" verse that we have just discussed, where the *samā'* in the singular applies to the seven heavens. It is important to point out though that the Qur'an's usage of the singular *samā'* to mean a plurality of heavens is by no means arbitrary. Its usage is contextual, and the context is dictated by ontological and cosmological considerations. This means that it is not sufficient on the basis of linguistic consideration alone to conclude that the usage of *samā'* in a particular verse is meant as a singular or as a plural.

For this reason, we sought to identify as precisely as possible the cosmological and ontological context of the application of the word *samā'* in the "third occurrence" verse (2:29). This verse is in a good position to serve as a basis of comparison with the other verses in which *al-samā'* occurs in the singular form, since this word in it is explicitly identified with the seven heavens. However, it is our contention that there are more profound aspects to the identification of *al-samā'* with *al-samāwāt* meaning-wise than the purely linguistic that can only be well-understood if the structure and shape of

---

51. Edward W. Lane, *Arabic-English Lexicon*, vol. 1, p. 1434.

the heavens were to be discussed in relation with the shape of the planet Earth. Actually, there is a close analogy between the identification of *al-samā'* with *al-samāwāt* to signify the same whole firmament and the identification of *al-'ālam* with *al-'ālamīn* to signify the same whole cosmos as previously discussed. Accordingly, we shall discuss later the issue of the structure and shape of the heavens together with that of the shape of the planet Earth.

Lexicologists of the Qur'an seem to have found its linguistic definition of *samā'*, on the basis of which the legitimacy of its use as a plural is upheld. This linguistic definition conforms to the Qur'an's ontological and cosmological teachings. We observe that, as in the case of its many other key terms,[52] the Qur'an has "Islamized" the semantic field of *samā'* in pre-Islamic Arabic to conform it to its worldview and conception of the heavens without, however, doing away with the word's core ideas and symbolic value that its users have understood and accepted for ages since the pre-Islamic period. Since this linguistic definition of *samā'* explains and justifies its use as a plural in the Qur'an, which in turn proves important to our understanding of all the 310 verses in which the word *samā'* occurs, both as a singular and as a plural, it would be a useful idea if we were to state the definition here and briefly explain the epistemological basis of the idea of *samā'* in Arabic usage that leads to the wide acceptance of the above linguistic

---

52. A modern scholar who has dealt extensively with the theme of the Qur'anic transformation of the semantics of pre-Islamic Arabic language, albeit with a concentration on a set of what he calls Qur'anic key-terms, see Toshihiko Izutsu, *God and Man in the Qur'an: Semantics of the Qur'anic Weltanschauung* (Tokyo: Keio University, 1964); also (Kuala Lumpur: Islamic Book Trust, 2002 new edition).

definition.

We owe the definition to al-Rāghib al-Iṣfahānī: "every *samā'* is a *samā'* with regard to what is below it."[53] The core idea in the word *samā'* is "that which is above or beyond something or someone." The word *samā'* thus serves as a very useful spatial symbol, because it is equated with the idea of "a certain kind of place" as indicated by the preposition "above." Prepositions such as above, below, inside, outside, in front, and behind are all spatial symbols. These spatial symbols are used widely in the Qur'an to depict spiritual positions. As generally explained in the lexicons and dictionaries, the word *samā'* is derived from the root word *samā'*, which conveys the core idea of "someone or something was or became high, lofty, raised, upraised, uplifted, up-reared, exalted, or elevated; it rose, or rose high."[54] Thus, the noun *samā'* carries the meaning of "the higher, or upper, or highest, or uppermost part of anything."[55]

Quite clearly, there are many objects having this very general meaning. A specific category of *samā'* was thus defined so as to distinguish it from the other objects sharing this general meaning. This category comprises anything that is spread like a canopy **above** any other thing. Because of its canopy-like shape that is spread above the earth, the visible sky clearly fits into this category of *samā'*. The visible sky is thus referred to in ordinary human language as the canopy of the earth. The Qur'an, however, does not limit the use of the word

53. See Abū'l-Qāsim Ḥusayn al-Rāghib al-Iṣfahānī, *Al-Mufradāt fī Gharīb al-Qur'ān* (Lebanon: Dar al-Ma'rifah, 2001).

54. Edward Lane, *Arabic-English Lexicon*, vol. 1, p. 1433.

55. Edward Lane, *Arabic-English Lexicon*, vol. 1, p. 1434.

*samā'* to signify the visible sky with its various functional roles in serving mankind, including the canopy-function.[56] It broadens the semantic field of this word so as to conform both in shape and function to its whole vision of the cosmos. The idea of several firmaments existing one above another (*ṭibāqan*), as mentioned in verse 67:3 and some other verses in the Qur'an, is a core dimension of the Qur'anic cosmos.

This Qur'anic idea means that a *samā'* can serve as a *samā'* to another *samā'* below it till the lowest *samā'* is reached, which is another way of expressing the linguistic definition of *samā'*, "every *samā'* is a *samā'* with regard to what is below it." This definition thus finds scriptural support in the Qur'an. It is also implied by the basic idea of *samā'* understood as "that canopy-like thing above another thing." When the idea is applied successively to a number of layers of canopy-like things, we will have a clear basis for the definition of *samā'*. However, the application of the idea of *samā'* to the heavens could only be inspired by Divine revelation. With the above understanding of the word *samā'* and its core relational idea of "above" serving as a spatial symbol, we would be able to better comprehend the meaning of firmament in the context of the verse on the expansion of the firmament (51:47).

In our earlier brief discussion of the "second occurrence" verse, we maintain that *al-samā'* as canopy ought to be distinguished from *al-samā'* as source of rain on the textual basis that it is referring to two different functions. While

---

56. *The Qur'an*, chapter 2 ("The Cow"), verse 22: "Who has made the Earth your couch, and the firmament (*al-samā'*) your canopy." In chapter 5, we will refer to some other verses concerning the heavens functioning as a canopy for mankind.

arguing for the interpretation of *al-samā'* as meaning the whole firmament, we did not have as of yet solid arguments to support the interpretation. In the light of the guiding principle derived from the "third occurrence" verse – a well-defined cosmological context for interpreting *al-samā'* as a plural – we may now proceed to show that the "second occurrence" verse, when read together with both its immediate preceding (2:21) and succeeding (2:23) verses, has meanings that are comparable in their cosmic dimension to the defining cosmological context of this principle. These three verses refer to at least three fundamental cosmic issues, namely the creation of mankind and their servitude to God (2:21), the creation of the Earth and the heaven (*al-samā'*) to serve mankind (2:22), and the descent of the Qur'an from the Divine Presence to the Prophet Muḥammad (May God's salutation and peace be upon him!) through the whole cosmos.

The Opening Chapter affirms the truth that mankind is central to God's creation and worship (*'ibadāh*) is the purpose of man's creation. Given all these facts pertaining to the cosmic dimension of the messages in the three verses, the earth and the *samā'* (2:22) must be understood as referring to the whole cosmos. Moreover, for the Earth to be the planetary home of man, God's most noble creation, the function of *al-samā'* as man's canopy has to embrace its protective role. However, as we shall further explain in our coming larger work the function of the heavens as cosmic roofs in protecting man from dangers and haphazard from outer space, the protective function is assumed by several layers of the firmament, and not just by the lowest *samā*.' The cosmic dimension of *al-samā'* in verse 2:22 may also be inferred from the textual fact that the ideas contained in this verse and verse 2:21 are actually explanations of the fundamental ideas *rabb al-ʿālamīn* ("the Lord of the worlds") and *īyāka naʾbudu wa īyāka nastaʾīn* ("Thou alone we worship, and Thou alone whose help we seek") in the opening chapter.

On the basis of the various arguments presented above, we may assert that the "second occurrence" verse (2:22) has the whole cosmos in view. Admittedly, the cosmic context of this verse is not as broad as that of the "third occurrence" verse, since it pertains to the more specific cosmic functions of the firmament as a canopy and of the earth as a couch, whereas the latter pertains to the wider dimensions of cosmic reality. Nonetheless, the functions envisaged still concern the whole cosmos. The cosmos envisaged in verse 2:22 comprises the planet Earth and the whole firmament which, as maintained by the "third occurrence" verse (2:29), consists of seven heavens understood as a perfect unified heavenly system with subsystems. The idea of a unified heavenly system is clearly conveyed by the statement "His design comprehended (*istawā*) the whole firmament (*al-samāʾ*) for He fashioned them (*sawwāhun*) into the seven heavens" (2:29). And the system is perfect as symbolized by the number seven. The perfection of this unified system is confirmed by the verse 67:3: "He Who created the seven heavens one above another: no want of proportion will you see in the creation of [God] the Most Gracious. So turn your vision again: do you see any flaw?" The idea of a perfect unified heavenly system as consisting of subsystems symbolized by the seven heavens furnishes the cosmological justification for the linguistic possibility of understanding *al-samāʾ* and *al-samāwāt* as both signifying all the firmaments as a contrast to the Earth.

There is also a metaphysical-theological argument

affirming the idea of a perfect heavenly system as consisting of a plurality of sub-heavenly systems. The verse 2:29 ends with this statement: "And of all things He has perfect knowledge." God's Attribute and Quality displayed in this verse is *'Alīm* ("The Omniscient"). Three Divine Acts are mentioned in the verse: *khalaqa* in relation to the creation of all things on the Earth for mankind; *istawā* in relation to the comprehensive design for all the heavens; and *sawwā* in relation to the fashioning of the seven heavens. All the three activities are knowledge activities. The last two activities pertain to the planning, designing, and fashioning the structures and shapes of the heavens. In this verse, the act of *khalaqa* was applied to the Earth. Al-Ghazzālī explains that God's act of *khalaqa* in manifesting His Quality of *Khāliq* ("Creator") is the act of planning and designing. Planning and designing involves the knowledge of *al-Khāliq* as a *muqaddir*[57] who determines the measures and proportions of all things and the precise relations between them, both qualitative and quantitative. In this case, the focus of the planning and designing is the planet Earth. Then God extends the planning and designing to the firmament (*thumma istawā ilā'l-samā'*).

His act of planning and designing the heavens is followed by His act of fashioning the seven heavens (*sawwāhun*). It is God as *al-Muṣawwir* "The Fashioner") that performs this act of fashioning. *Muṣawwir* also means a giver of forms. So as applied to the firmament (*al-samā'*), God as *al-Muṣawwir* fashioned it into the seven heavens by giving them forms (sing:

57. Al-Ghazzālī, *The Ninety-Nine Beautiful Names of God*, p. 68.

*ṣūrah*) and arranging these forms in the finest way.[58] The word "form" (*ṣūrah*) can mean a number of things. However, when it comes to the heavens, the dominant forms are mathematical or astronomical in nature. These mathematical forms refer to the shapes and figures of the heavens as signified by the term *hay'ah*.[59] Astronomy is interested in studying the mathematical shapes of the heavens. For this reason, the term *'ilm al-hay'ah* is often used in traditional Islamic science to denote astronomy understood as the study of the shapes of the heavens. Thus, since all the three Divine acts mentioned in the verse are essentially concerned with knowledge, it is God's Quality of the All-Knowing that solely features in it. In the light of the above discussion, we may describe the "third occurrence" verse as of great significance to science, particularly astronomy.

The "second and third occurrences" verses together provide a wealth of information in a concise and essential summary form about the shape and functions of the Earth and the heavens. The idea of "the earth as a couch (*firāsh*)" (2:22) and the idea of the earth "providing all the needs of man" (2:29) allude to the shape and function of the Earth. The idea of "the firmament (*al-samā'*) as a canopy (*binā'*)" (2:22) and the idea of God's "extending His design to the whole firmament (*al-samā'*)" and "fashioning the seven heavens" (2:29) also pertain

---

58. For an explanation of the role of God as The Fashioner and Giver of Forms (*Al-Muṣawwir*), see al-Ghazzālī, *The Ninety-Nine Beautiful Names of God*, pp. 68-69.

59. In their discussion of the subject of form (*ṣūrah*) and matter (*maddah*), classical Muslim scientists and philosophers often used the term *hay'ah* to signify mathematical forms and shapes as distinct from the general meaning of shape (*khilqah*) and form (*ṣūrah*).

to the shape and function of the heavens. We have just provided a preliminary discussion of the possible meanings of the structure and shapes of the heavens that are indicated in the verse. This discussion shows that scientific knowledge in astronomy, especially of the modern era, would help provide a more detailed explanation of the structure and the shapes of the heavens, especially as viewed from the planet Earth, since the Qur'anic view of the cosmos is basically "geocentric."

However, as we will be able to see later, the Qur'anic "geocentric" view of the cosmos should by no means be equated with the medieval geocentric view of the world that was overthrown by the Copernican revolution in European science. The geocentric perspective of the Qur'an connotes a different cosmological meaning and moreover, it is flexible enough, conceptually speaking, to integrate modern astronomical knowledge of real worth into its body of knowledge about the cosmos. In our present times, thanks to a rapid advancement in our astronomical knowledge, it has become meaningless to speak of the "center" of the cosmos in an absolute sense. The existence of several solar systems and galaxies other than our own can only make the idea of the center of the cosmos a relative one.

In order to arrive at a more cohesive view of the cosmos as seen from man's position on the Earth, we will now discuss the issue of the structure and the shapes of the heavens without separating it from that of the planet Earth. However, apart from the "second and third occurrences" verses, we will bring into the discussion some other relevant verses that will help furnish a clearer astronomical picture of the cosmos. In particular, we are bringing into the discussion the verse on the "seven layers of the heavens one above another" (67:3) and the verse on the "expansion of the firmament (*al-samā'*)" (51:47). Because of their relevance, the verses that immediately follow 67:3 and 51:47 are also included for discussion. The included verse 67:5 reads: "And We have adorned (*zayyanna*) the lowest heaven (*al-samā' al-dunyā*) with lamps (*maṣābīh*), and We have made such [lamps] [as] missiles to drive away the Evil Ones (*al-shayāṭin*)." And the other included verse 51:48 reads: "And We have spread out (*farashnā*) the Earth: how excellently We do spread out!"

In the light of our foregoing discussion on the "second and third occurrences" verses, we are now able to interpret the firmament (*al-samā'*) that is expanding (51:47) as signifying the whole firmament consisting of the seven heavens. In other words, the whole cosmic space enclosing the Earth is expanding. The notion of an expanding cosmos is not yet fully understood. On the basis of our current understanding of the Qur'an, we do not see it somewhere in its verses explaining this interesting phenomenon of cosmic expansion. However, going by the Qur'anic principle that its verses explain each other, we cannot rule out the possibility that somewhere in the Sacred Text there are hints to the expansion phenomenon. For possible insights into the issue we may explore the semantic field of the verb forms related to the Divine Quality *al-Wāsi'* ("The Vast and All-Encompassing") and the verbal noun *mūsi'un*, since the latter is the precise word that appears in the "expansion" verse (51:47).

The Divine Name *Al-Wāsi'* is very pertinent in this case. In accordance with Ibn al-'Arabī's theory of the cosmos and its phenomena viewed as God's self-disclosure, the Divine Quality *al-Wāsi'* must manifest or display itself in the cosmos among others through its property of vastness.[60] The idea of vastness is to be understood both in the spiritual and physical sense. The Qur'an refers to vastness in the spiritual sense in this verse: "...verily your Lord is vast and all-embracing (*wāsi'*) in forgiveness."[61] Our concern here, however, is with physical vastness. And we know how vast the cosmos is, just on the basis of what modern astronomy is presently telling us. Our planet Earth is about 93 million miles from the Sun around which it revolves in approximately 365 days. The furthest planet of our solar system from the Sun is Pluto, which is 40 times the distance from the Earth to the Sun. In other words, Pluto is about 3720 million miles away from the Sun. So the furthest distance from one end of the solar system to the other is approximately 7440 million miles. But our solar system, already of a staggering size from the human point of view, is only a small portion of the gigantic stellar system called "the Milky Way galaxy." A galaxy is usually defined as a large system of stars, gas, and dust held together by mutual gravitation. Modern astronomy has discovered billions of galaxies in the observable cosmos, and these galaxies are isolated from each other by vast regions of space. The galaxies are of different sizes, but a typical galaxy is made up of billions of stars. Our

---

60. The quality *wāsi'* in reference to God is mentioned 9 times in the Qur'an. In 8 out of these occurrences, the word *wāsi'* is mentioned together with the divine quality of knowing (*'alīm*) (7 times) or the divine quality of wise (*ḥakīm*) (once) to convey the primary meaning of God as the All-Encompassing. In the ninth occurrence (chapter 53, verse 32), it is perhaps more appropriate to interpret *wāsi* as "vast," meaning that there the Divine Quality that is the focus of man's attention is "The Vast." However, in all these occurrences, the noun *wāsi'* does not refer to the physical cosmos.

61. *The Qur'an*, chapter 53 ("The Star"), verse 32.

own galaxy, the Milky Way, is made up of a hundred billion stars and many solar systems.

The cosmic space is vaster than what is depicted above. The Qur'an gives a metaphysical explanation of this cosmic vastness. Since one of God's Names is "The Vast" (*Al-Wāsi'*), which is of course to be understood in the absolute sense, the properties and effects of this Quality are found in the cosmos He created. As the Vast, God's activity in creation is to extend and expand the cosmic space (*innā la-mūsi'ūn*). This Divine activity has the effect of imparting an "extensive and expansive" nature to cosmic space. The extensive and expansive dimension of the cosmic space is shown by the fact that it is continuously expanding. This metaphysically motivated understanding of the expansion of cosmic space has important implications for the modern scientific debate between the "big bang" theory and the "steady state" theory[62] concerning the origin of the physical cosmos and the underlying causes of its expansion. Currently, both theories accept cosmic expansion as a "fact"; and both call for "space" to be spontaneously created "in between" galaxies. By expansion is meant the moving away of the galaxies from one another.

The main dispute between the two theories pertains to their explanations of the causes of the expansion. The big bang

---

62. In simple terms, the big bang theory posits a belief in the single origin of the cosmos in order to account for the cosmic expansion. The steady state theory is based on the fundamental belief that the cosmos is essentially uniform in space and time, which means a denial of the origin and the end of the cosmos. Most scientists today favour the big bang theory, arguing that it is more tenable on scientific grounds. Since both theories have implications for beliefs in God as the Creator of the cosmos, religious people tend to favour the big bang theory.

theory attributes the expansion to the continuous and lasting effect of a cosmic event in the far distant past that gave birth to the cosmos.[63] The steady state theory on the other hand attributes the expansion to the continuous bubbling up of the element hydrogen from "empty space" at a constant rate that scientists have determined. It is this slowly accumulated hydrogen over time that eventually condenses into stars. This theory therefore seeks to explain cosmic expansion in terms of the continuous creation of new matter that it believes does not result in any significant change to the general appearance of the cosmos, because the phenomena of the birth and the death of stars will go on repeating themselves indefinitely.

Despite having acquired a wealth of new astronomical data, modern man does not yet have a clear and coherent picture of the physical heavens. By themselves, these scientific data even if they are empirically established, could not furnish a coherent astronomical picture of the cosmos. These data need to be integrated into a larger cosmological framework, within which alone they acquire certainty and epistemologically become most meaningful. Only Divine revelation could provide this larger unifying framework that would be comprehensive, holistic and synthetic enough to undertake the task of conceptual integration. As the revelation of *tawḥīd* par excellence, the Qur'an would be better equipped epistemologically than any other sacred scripture to provide such a unifying framework. Further, in our view, it is the

63. Scientists who accept this theory in general terms differ among themselves on the details of the "original event" and their detailed explanations of it have undergone rapid changes since the theory was first developed in the late 1920s.

Qur'anic model of the cosmos viewed as God's Self-Disclosure (*tajallī*) as developed by Ibn al-'Arabī[64] and his school that could best address the various contentious issues among scientists concerning the origin, nature, and development of the physical cosmos from an independent metaphysical perspective.

For example, some astronomers raise the pertinent question of the beginning of the cosmic expansion. They want to know whether or not the expansion presently observed has been an integral feature of the cosmos right from its beginning. Some astronomers affirm that the expansion phenomenon has indeed taken place from the beginning of the cosmos. From the perspective of God's Self-Disclosure (GSD) model, cosmic expansion is one of the traces (*āthār*) and properties (*aḥkām*) of the Divine Name and Quality of *Al-Wāsi'* in the cosmos. In other words, expansion is a physical property of the cosmos, meaning that the cosmos has been displaying this property from the beginning of its history. The model would therefore affirm the admissibility of any empirical evidence of cosmic expansion being integrated into its general view of the astronomical picture of the heavens. However, any claim that cosmic space is a static or constant thing or that it would revert to its previous contraction phase after having reached the terminal point of its present expansion phase, as maintained by some proponents of the steady state theory, would be contrary to the GSD model.

The idea that the Divine Quality *Al-Wāsi'* only enters into a

---

64. For an excellent explanation of Ibn al-'Arabī's divine self-disclosure model, see William C. Chittick, *The Self-Disclosure of God: Principles of Ibn al-'Arabī's Cosmology* (Albany: SUNY Press, 1998), pp.52-57.

relationship with the cosmos at some point later in the evolution of the cosmos would imply that the Quality in view is subject to the requirements of time and space. This, a Divine Quality could not be. Although just like any other Divine Quality, the Quality *al-Wāsi‘* displays traces and properties in the world of time and space, It is independent of them. In like manner, we may apply the GSD model to the discussion of other issues related to the cosmic expansion such as the spontaneous creation of matter or space "in between" the galaxies and the orderly nature of each of the galaxies as an astronomical system. However, certain constraints related to this work do not allow us to undertake such discussions.

We have discussed at length the issue of cosmic expansion raised by the verse 51:47 when it refers to God's activity of expanding the firmament (*al-samā'*), because it is fundamentally related to the issue of the astronomical picture of the cosmos viewed in its widest sense. We have already seen how in treating the "expansion of the firmament," we were led to viewing a vast astronomical picture in which we could see beyond our own solar system other astronomical systems in our Milky Way galaxy and billions of other galaxies. There are other aspects and dimensions of the astronomical picture of the cosmos that we touched briefly earlier but shall now discuss in greater details. A dimension featuring prominently in the Qur'an is the Earth-centric vision of the structure and shapes of the heavens, which is closely related to man's position on the planet Earth and the Earth's relationship with the rest of the cosmos.

In addressing the issue of man's vision of the cosmos relative to his own position on earth, the Qur'an presents both how the planet Earth and the rest of the cosmos, namely the firmaments, appear to him. In a number of verses, the Qur'an describes the Earth as a "spread out" that is signified by several different words. Altogether, there are five such words occurring in the Qur'an, either in their verb or noun forms: *firāshan* ("as a spread"), *farasha* ("to spread out"), *bisāṭan* ("as a spread out such as a carpet"), *madadnā* ("we have spead out"), *māhidūn* ("spreaders"), and *suṭiḥat* ("it is spread out"). The words *firāshan* and *farasha* each occur only once in the Qur'an.[65] The two verses read: "Who has made the Earth your spread out (*firāshan*)" (2:22);[66] and "We have spread out (*farashna*) the Earth" (51:48).[67] The word *bisāṭan*, which occurs only once in

---

65. There are only four other verses in the Qur'an that are derived from the root verb of the first form (*farasha*), but none of them occurs in connection with the Earth. However, in two verses, the word *furush* (sing: *firāsh*) is used to mean "carpets" (55:54) and "spouses" (56:34). Exegetes such as al-Baghawī, Zamakhsharī, al-Rāzī, Bayḍāwī, and Muhammad Asad interpret *furush* in 56:34 as "spouses," while Yusuf 'Ali interprets it as "thrones."

66. The noun *firāsh* (pl: *furush*) may refer to specific items that make up bedroom furniture such as bed or couch, mattress, cushion and pillow, or to any kind of spread. Its core idea thus pertains either to its functional aspect as indicated by the bedroom furniture items or to the idea of the spread out as an allusion to its real nature and shape. As applied to the planet Earth, as sought to be contrasted with the firmament, we believe it would be more appropriate in the present context of our discussion about man's vision of his own planet and his vision of the heavens to translate *firāsh* as ("spread out").

67. There is a subtle difference between the main idea in the noun *firāsh* ("a spread"), which is the result of the act of spreading out, and the main idea in the verb *farasha* ("to spread out"), which is the act itself, especially with reference to the Earth. In reference to the noun form, as in 2:22, the emphasis is on the functional role of the product of spreading out. In reference to the verb form, as in 51:48, the emphasis is on the nature of the

the Qur'an and in connection with the Earth, is derived from the root word *basaṭa*. The verse reads: "And God has made the Earth for you as a "spread out" (*bisāṭan*)."[68] The root word *basaṭa* conveys the meaning of "to spread out, to flatten, to unfold or to unroll" something. All these meanings allude to the shape of the object that is being "spread out." The word *madadnā* ("we have spread out") occurs in this verse: "And the Earth We have spread out (*madadnāhā*) [like a carpet]."[69] Its root verb *madda* has the core meaning of "to spread out, stretch out, and lay out." There are 13 occurrences in the Qur'an of this verb form, but only four of them pertain directly to the Earth. One of these four verses has just been cited (15:19). The other verses (V1, V2, V3) are the following:

> V1: And it is He Who spread out (*madda*) the earth, and set thereon mountains standing firm and [flowing] rivers...[70]

---

act of spreading out in relation to the object that is being "spread out." That it is the supra-human and miraculous nature of the spreading out that is sought to be emphasized in this verse is clear from its last portion and its comparison with the immediate preceding and succeeding verses. The last portion of 51:48 reads: "... how excellently We do spread out (*ni'ma al-māhidūn*)!" The immediate preceding verse is about God's power and skill in constructing the heavens and expanding (51:47); the immediate succeeding verse is about the creation of all things in pairs, which furnish traditional Islamic science with the important idea of "the pairing principle." The verse reads: "And of everything We have created pairs (*zawjayn*): that you may receive instruction" (51:49).

68. *The Qur'an*, chapter 71 ("Noah"), verse 19.

69. *The Qur'an*, chapter 15 ("The Rocky Tracts"), verse 19.

70. *The Qur'an*, chapter 13 ("The Thunder"), verse 3.

To better appreciate the textual context of this verse (V1) we mention here both its immediate preceding and succeeding verses. Its preceding verse reads: "God is He Who raised the heavens (*al-samāwāt*) without any pillars that you can see; is firmly established on the Throne [of Authority] (*istawā 'alā'l-'arsh*). He has subjected the sun and the moon [to His Law]! Each one runs [its course] for a term appointed."[71] And here is its succeeding verse: "And in the earth are tracts [diverse though] neighboring, and gardens of vines and fields sown with corn, and palm trees..." (13:4). Quite clearly, the context shows that the verse V1 seeks to highlight the kind of skill and perfection that goes into the Divine Act of spreading out the Earth that is comparable to His construction of the heavens without observable pillars and the creation of orderly systems of celestial bodies.

> V2: And the Earth We have spread it out (*madadnāhā*) and set thereon mountains standing firm, and produced therein every kind of beautiful growth in pairs.[72]

Again with the view of having a better appreciation of the context of this verse (V2) as well, we cite here its immediate preceding and succeeding verses. Its preceding verse reads: "Do they not look at the firmament (*al-samā'*) above them? – how We have constructed (*banaynā*) it and adorned (*zayyannā*) it, and there are no flaws (*furūj*)?[73] in it?"(50:6). The succeeding

71. *The Qur'an*, chapter 13 ("The Thunder"), verse 2.

72. *The Qur'an*, chapter 50 ("Qāf"), verse 7.

73. In note 11 the word "flaw" was also used to translate *fuṭūr* in connection with the claim made in verse 67:3 that God's construction of the seven heavens one above another is a perfect work without any flaw. In this verse,

verse reads: "To be a source of insight (*tabṣiratan*) and a reminder (*dhikrā*) to every human being who willingly turns (*'abdin munībin*) [unto God]" (50:8). The textual context of the verse V2 clearly shows that the Divine Act of spreading out the Earth alludes to some aspects of its unique nature and physical reality that call for comparison with the "flawless" construction of the firmament. The adornment of the firmament with beautiful light emitting bodies is to be compared with the adornment of the Earth with beautiful growths and other living forms. The succeeding verse (50:8) that invites man to reflect on the spreading out of the Earth and its adornment provides clear proof that there is something special about the reality of the planet that God wants man to find out by himself.

V3: And when the Earth is flattened out (*muddat*).

The verses preceding V3 read: "When the sky (*al-samā'*) is rent asunder, and listens to [the command of] its Lord and its new reality is fulfilled (*ḥuqqat*)" (84:1-2). The succeeding verse says: "And casts forth what is within it and becomes [clean] empty" (84:4). We see that the context of the verse V3 is

---

however, the word *furūj* is used. As we see it, different words with slightly different meanings are used, because the reference to the possibility of any flaw in the Divine work made in the two cases concerns different aspects and dimensions of the heavens. The issue of *fuṭūr* was appropriately raised in the case of the construction of the seven heavens, because the core idea of *fuṭūr* is about cracks, fissures, and ruptures that we normally associate with flaws in finished construction works. In the present case, the word *furūj* would be the appropriate one to be used to refer to any flaw, because the product that is to be evaluated is not just the construction of the heavens but also its adornment. The idea of gaps and openings conveyed by the word *furūj* is quite apt to be applied to possible flaws and defects in the adornment of the heavens.

entirely different from previous contexts which were all almost similar in their main messages and points of emphasis. This time, the context pertains to the eschatological event of the end of the world as we know it. In verse V3, the spreading or flattening out of the Earth is no longer an "apparent reality" for man but a true reality. The Earth has become real flat, because it has been emptied of its whole content as made clear by the succeeding verse 84:4. Ever since man lives on earth, it appears to him as a spread out or as flat, but in reality it is a spherical body. It is its content, which science knows very little, that preserves its sphericity. The moment it is emptied of its content, it becomes totally flat just like when a fully blown balloon is emptied of its air content.

We know now that the Earth is spherical in shape. We can see with our own naked eye its real shape in pictures taken from outer space. Many classical Muslim scientists knew that the Earth is a spherical body through established rational and scientific arguments on the basis of evidences made available by the conditions of the Earth itself and the rest of the observable cosmos. But rational certainty of the mind arrived at through logical inferences, which the Qur'an refers to as *'ilm al-yaqīn*, is weaker in quality than certainty of sight (*'ayn al-yaqīn*).[74] Modern scientific knowledge enables us to know the

---

74. The Qur'an refers to three different levels of certainty that are within the reach of human experience. In their ascending order of "excellence" the levels are *'ilm al-yaqīn* ("inferential certainty"), *'ayn al-yaqīn* ("certainty of sight"), and *ḥaqq al-yaqīn* ("certainty of truth"). The phrases *'ilm al-yaqīn* and *'ayn al-yaqīn* are mentioned together in Chapter *al-Takāthur* ("The Piling Up") in these verses: "Nay, were you to know with certainty of mind (*'ilm al-yaqīn*) [you would beware!]" (102:5); and "Again, you shall see it with certainty of sight (*'ilm al-yaqīn*)" (102:7). The phrase *ḥaqq al-yaqīn* is

real shape of the Earth with the certainty of sight. All the previous verses about the spreading out of the Earth are aimed at leading man from its apparent reality to its true reality so that in knowing both its real shape and its unique features as a spread out he will understand the dominant Divine Qualities which these physical realities disclose. The "third occurrence" verse discloses the Divine Names and Qualities of *al-Khāliq* ("The Planner-Designer-Creator"), *al-Muṣawwir* ("The Originator of Forms and the Fashioner"), and *al-'Alīm* ("The All-Knowing"): "It is He Who created (*khalaqa*) for you all things that are on earth; ... extends His design (*istawā*) to the firmament; then He fashioned (*sawwa*) them into the seven heavens; and He is the All-Knowing (*bi-kull shay'in 'alīm*)" (2:29). Man's knowledge of these Divine Names and Qualities – and others – through knowledge of God's "spreading out" of the Earth is what is intended by the verses 50:7-8: "And the Earth We have spread it out ... to be a source of enlightenment (*tabṣirat*) and spiritual reminder (*dhikrā*) for every servant who wants to turn back to God (*'abdin munībin*)."

The certainty of physical vision that we have concerning the real physical shape of the Earth made possible by modern technology has brought a new significance to our understanding of the qur'anic verses about the "spreading out" of the Earth in its manifold dimensions as well as about the geocentric pictures of the shapes of the heavens. The increase in scientific knowledge about the planet Earth and its cosmic position and significance in relation to other planets in our

---

mentioned in two verses. Verse 95 in chapter 56 ("The Inevitable Event") says: "Verily, this is the certainty of truth (*ḥaqq al-yaqīn*)." This verse is almost repeated in chapter 69 ("The Sure Reality"), verse 51.

own solar system and to the rest of the cosmos has not rendered these verses scientifically irrelevant or obsolete. The statements made in these verses are as true today as it was when they were first revealed, whether we are viewing the Earth from our position on its surface or from a far distance in outer space. In fact, our physical vision of the Earth as a very large spherical body of planetary size only enhances our appreciation of the scientific as well as the metaphysical significance of these verses.

Mathematically, scientifically, architecturally, and technologically speaking, the creation of a spherical body with the right radius or size and surface conditions that can best project its appearance as a "spread out" to man and sustain the needs of its occupants can only be described as a supernatural or supra-human feat. The act of spreading out a spherical body of the Earth's size without the slightest reduction in its sphericity could be attributed only to God, and this is the perennial message conveyed by the "spreading out of the Earth" verses. And God says, "How excellently We do spread out (51:48)." However, science can help us to better understand and appreciate the vast knowledge that must go into this creative act of "spreading out the Earth" and also to gain new knowledge about the content within the spherical body of the Earth.

The fact that the Earth is a spherical body has consequences for man's vision of the heavens. We have been told that the whole firmament (*al-samā'*) above the surface of the Earth comprises the seven heavens one above another.[75] Since the

---

75. The phrase "seven heavens" occurs seven times in the Qur'an. But the description that they are "one above another" (*ṭibāqan*) is only found in two

Earth is spherical, albeit not perfectly so, it is enclosed by all the firmaments, each of which functioning as a spherical layer with the Earth as the common center. In other words, the Earth becomes the center of a system of concentric spherical layers corresponding to the different levels of the firmament. This multi-layered structure of the heavens was adopted by classical Muslim astronomers and philosophers as the astronomical representation of the whole cosmos. As previously emphasized, in reference to the seven heavens, the number seven is understood not as a quantity but a symbol of perfect plurality. Thus, classical Muslim astronomers used a different number of heavens to depict the whole cosmos. For example, for both theoretical and practical considerations, *Ikhwān al-Ṣafā'* adopted an astronomical system symbolized by nine heavens to depict the cosmos.[76] Each heaven is identified with a particular physical celestial body that functions as its visible symbol, except the eighth and the ninth heavens each symbolized by a stellar system. The first or lowest heaven is identified with the Moon, which is usually not regarded as a planet but as a satellite of the planet Earth. The second and third heavens have Mercury and Venus respectively as their planetary symbols.

The fourth heaven is symbolized by the Sun, which is the only star in our solar system, since it is the only self-luminous body to be found within the system. The fifth, sixth and seven heavens have Mars, Jupiter, and Saturn as their respective planetary symbols. The eighth heaven is symbolized by the

---

verses, namely chapter 67, verse 3 and chapter 71, verse 15, both of which have been previously cited.

76. See Seyyed Hossein Nasr, *An Introduction to Islamic Cosmological Doctrines*, p. 76-77.

fixed stars. Unlike the previous heavens, this heaven does not have a single body as its physical symbol, but rather a constellation of fixed stars (*al-kawākib al-thābita*). According to Ikhwān al-Ṣafā', the stars are self-luminous, spherical bodies. Seven of them are wandering, but the rest stationary. In their attempt to conform to Qur'anic cosmology, Ikhwān al-Ṣafā' equated the heaven of the fixed stars with the "Pedestal" or "Seat" (*kursī*) mentioned in this verse: "His Pedestal encompasses the heavens and the Earth…"[77] The ninth heaven is the outermost sphere of the cosmos, and is thus referred to as the *Muḥīṭ*.[78] Inasmuch as they locate the signs of the Zodiac in the *Muḥīṭ*, we may speak of the ninth heaven being symbolized by these Zodiac signs. Ikhwān al-Ṣafā' equated the ninth heaven with the Divine "Throne" (*'arsh*) that is mentioned 22 times in the Qur'an. Examples are the following two verses: "God is He Who raised the heavens without any pillars extending it to as high up as the Throne (*al-'arsh*);"[79] and "And the angels will be on its sides, and eight will, that Day, bear the Throne of your Lord (*'arsh rabbik*) above them."[80]

Ibn Sīnā also adopted a nine-heaven model of the cosmos, but his terminological description of the eighth and the ninth heavens differs from that of *Ikhwān al-Ṣafā'*. He called the

77. *The Qur'an*, chapter 2 ("The Cow"), verse 255.

78. Seyyed Hossein Nasr, *Introduction to Islamic Cosmological Doctrines*, p. 76.

79. *The Qur'an*, chapter 13 ("The Thunder"), verse 2.

80. *The Qur'an*, chapter 69 ("The Sure Reality"), verse 17.

eighth heaven *falak al-burūj*,[81] which may best translated as "the heaven of the constellation of fixed stars." The ninth heaven he named *falak al-aflāk* ("the heaven of heavens"), which is starless. The word *burūj* occurs 4 times in the Qur'an. Except in one verse, all its occurrences pertain to the whole firmament. The most representative of these verses in conveying the meaning of *burūj* as intended by the context is the following: "It is We Who have positioned constellations (*burūj*) in the firmament (*al-samā'*) and endowed them with beauty for all to behold."[82] Linguistically, the word *burūj* conveys among other things the meaning of constellations in general,[83] although it is also used to refer to specific constellations, especially the stars of the Zodiac. It would be more in conformity with the current state of astronomical knowledge and the general astronomical significance of the verse, if we were to translate *burūj* as "constellations." It is this more general cosmic meaning of the word *burūj* that is intended in this verse as well as in the other two verses. God swears "By the sky full of constellations! (*wa'l-samā' dhāt al-burūj*)" (85:1). At the moment, there are 88 constellations in the heavens that are visible to the naked eye.

Quite clearly, adopting a more general meaning of *burūj* as "constellation" would enhance the scientific significance of the three verses about "the *burūj* of the heavens" without in any

---

81. Seyyed Hossein Nasr, *Introduction to Islamic Cosmological Doctrines*, p. 204.

82. *The Qur'an*, chapter 15 ("The Rocky Tracts"), verse 16. For the other two verses, see chapter 25 ("The Criterion"), verse 61; and chapter 85 ("The Constellations"), verse 1.

83. Edward W. Lane, *Arabic-English Lexicon*, vol. 1, p. 180.

way compromising their spiritual significance. Muhammad Asad mentions the names of several Qur'anic exegetes such as al-Baghawī, Bayḍāwī, Ibn Kathīr, and Murtaḍā al-Zabīdī (d. 1205 A.H.) whose interpretation of *burūj* served as the basis of his own rendering of the word as "great constellations."[84]Yusuf 'Ali interprets *burūj* in verse 15:16 as "Zodiacal Signs,"[85] although in the other two verses (25:61 and 85:1) he translates it as "constellations." It is possible that his main consideration in rendering *burūj* as "Zodiacal Signs" is the allusion of the two succeeding verses to astrological practices, which are closely related to the issue of human beliefs about the meaning and significance of these signs for their personal lives. We contend, however, that notwithstanding the close connection between "zodiacal signs" and astrology, we can still deal with the "evil" dimension of the latter within the framework of a broader cosmic understanding of *burūj*.

Some classical Muslim astronomers explained the qur'anic idea of the physical heavens as being protected from "satanic forces" (*kull shayṭān rajīm*) with the cosmological argument that it is in the nature of the heavens to be "out of bound" to the "satanic forces." The nature of the latter is such that it is only in the sublunary region stretching from the Earth to the lowest heaven, namely the sphere of the moon, that they can exercise their power and influence. These astronomers identify this region as the world of generation and corruption in which

84. Muhammad Asad, *The Message of the Qur'an*, pp. 459-460.

85. 'Abdullah Yusuf 'Ali, *The Meaning of the Holy Qur'an*, p. 510.

the good and the evil coexist and interact.[86] While agreeing with this "cosmological" interpretation of the domain of "satanic forces" we advance another explanation of the connection between the heavenly constellations (*burūj*) and the "satanic forces." As it becomes clearer to us that it is not only our solar system that is orderly and well regulated by physical and mathematical laws that can be known by us with the certainty of *'ilm al-yaqīn*, but also the constellations (*burūj*), we can expect the celestial bodies and stellar systems in our Milky Way galaxy to increasingly reveal about their true identities and behaviors that can only frustrate all the astrological predictions made about them that are conjectural in nature (*al-rajm bi'l-ghayb*).

The astronomical model of the cosmos just discussed in which the Moon, the Sun, the planets of our solar system, the constellations, and the Divine Pedestals and Throne have their respective roles and functions to play, both physical and symbolic, are presented by its adopters as being in conformity with the Qur'an's cosmological data. Within this astronomical system that is to be viewed more as of a qualitative model of the cosmos rather than a quantitative one, the lowest heaven is identified with the sphere of the moon. In the light of this astronomical model of the cosmos adopted by the astronomers, it is necessary to pose the question whether or not it is possible to integrate the qur'anic idea of *al-samā' al-dunyā* into the model. The phrase *al-samā' al-dunyā* occurs thrice in the Qur'an. The first verse reads: "We have indeed adorned the

86. See, for example, the views of Ikhwān al-Ṣafā' on the cosmic domain of "satanic forces" in Seyyed Hossein Nasr, *Introduction to Islamic Cosmological Doctrines*, pp. 69-70, 84-95.

lower heavens (*al-samā' al-dunyā*) with the beauty of the stars (*zīnah al-kawākib*) and have made them as guard (*ḥifẓan*) against every obstinate rebellious evil spirit."[87] The second verse mentions *al-samā' al-dunyā* with a slight variation: "... We adorned the lower heavens with lights (*maṣābīḥ*) and [made it] well-guarded: such is the Decree of the Exalted in Might (*al-'Azīz*) and the All-Knowing (*al-'Alīm*)."[88] The third verse concerning *al-samā' al-dunyā* reads: "And We have adorned the lower heavens with lights (*maṣābīḥ*), and We have made such lights as missiles to drive away (*rujūman*) the evil ones..."[89]

In order to answer the question posed, it is necessary to establish the identity of *al-samā' al-dunyā* mentioned in the three verses. Noting that the word *dunyā* may be understood either in its superlative or comparative sense and that the word *samā'* may be used in its plural sense, we render the phrase *al-samā' al-dunyā* as "the lower heavens," meaning "the heavens nearer to us on earth." There are two-key words in the three verses that are crucial to our correct interpretation of this phrase, namely *kawākib* (sing: *kawkab*) and *maṣābīḥ* (sing: *miṣbāḥ*). According to the classical lexicons, the word *kawkab* is used to either refer to "stars" or "planets."[90] It is also used to

87. *The Qur'an*, chapter 37 ("Those Arranged in Ranks"), verses 6-7.

88. *The Qur'an*, chapter 41 ("Expounded"), verse 12.

89. *The Qur'an*, chapter 67 ("The Dominion"), verse 5.

90. Edward W. Lane, *Arabic-English Lexicon*, vol. 2, p. 2623. Lane points out that in classical Arabic usage, *al-kawkab* used to be one of the names of the planet Venus. The well-known astronomer, 'Abd al-Raḥman al-Ṣūfī (903 A. D. – 986 A. D.) titled one of his works, *Kitāb ṣuwar al-kawākib al-thābita* ("The Book on the Configuration of the Fixed Stars").

mean "constellation." If we are to interpret the meaning of *al-samā' al-dunyā* by just relying on the information about *kawākib* given in the first verse (37:6-7), ignoring the meanings of the adorning entities mentioned in the second and third verses, namely the *maṣābīḥ*, we would not be able to pinpoint the "lower heavens" that the Qur'an has in view. So we need to look at the meaning of *kawākib* that would be consistent with the meaning of *maṣābīḥ*. Since the stars are self-luminous bodies and the planets are not, it would be helpful to the identification of *al-samā' al-dunyā* if we can assign to which category of the celestial bodies the light-emitting bodies (*maṣābīḥ*) belong.

The classical lexicons tell us that *miṣbaḥ* is synonymous with *sirāj*,[91] which conveys the meaning of a self-burning or self-luminous lamp. In referring to the Sun as a *sirāj*, the Qur'an affirms its nature as a star or self-luminous body, as it is actually described by science. The word *sirāj* occurs four times in the Qur'an, but only once with an explicit reference to the Sun. This latter verse reads: "And [He] made the Moon a light (*nūran*) in their midst, and made the Sun as a Lamp (*sirājan*)."[92] However, it is quite clear that in two of the other verses (25:61; 78:13) the word *sirāj* is referring to the Sun, even though it is not explicitly mentioned there.[93] The Qur'an seeks

91. Edward W. Lane, *Arabic-English Lexicon*, vol. 2, p. 1643.

92. *The Qur'an*, chapter 71 ("Noah"), verse 16. For the other three verses, see chapter 25 ("The Criterion"), verse 61; chapter 33 ("The Confederates"), verse 46; and chapter 78 ("The Great News"), verse 13.

93. The only instance when the word *sirāj* occurs not in reference to the physical Sun but rather to the Prophet Muḥammad (May God's salutation and peace be upon him!) is this verse (33:46): "And [you O Prophet] as one

to distinguish between the nature and function of the Sun as *sirāj* and that of the Moon as *munīr* as in this verse: "Blessed is He Who made constellations (*burūj*) in the skies (*al-samā'*), and placed therein a Lamp (*sirājan*) and a giving-light Moon (*qamaran munīran*)."[94] To further highlight the distinction, the Qur'an mentions an additional feature of the Sun: "And We placed [therein the Sun] a lamp full of blazing splendor (*sirājan wahhājjan*)."[95] Modern scientific exegetes of the Qur'an try to explain the distinction in terms of fundamental differences in the nature and quality of light emitted by the two celestial bodies.[96]

The Sun is a star, since it is self-luminous and, in fact, it is the lone star in the solar system. The Moon does not have light of its own, but merely reflects the light that it receives from the Sun. The term *wahhājj* used by the Qur'an to describe the Sun conveys meanings that seem to confirm much of what modern science is telling us about this Star. The root word *wahaja* conveys the core meaning of "to blaze, burn, be incandescent, flame, be red-hot, and shine brilliantly." The adjective *wahhājj* embraces all these closely interrelated meanings, which are most apt to be attributed to the Sun. Science tells us that the Sun consumes its own fuel to burn and produce heat and light and to be in an incessant state of incandescence. The physical

---

who invites to God's [Grace] by His permission, and as a lamp (*sirājan*) spreading light (*munīran*)."

94. *The Qur'an*, chapter 25 ("The Criterion"), verse 61.

95. *The Qur'an*, chapter 78 ("The Great News"), verse 13.

96. See, for example, Maurice Bucaille, *The Bible, The Qur'an and Science*, pp. 155-156.

reality of a *sirāj* ("lamp") burning its own oil to light itself so that it will continue to glow as long as it is not emptied of its fuel is analogous to the Sun burning its own fuel to continuously shine brilliantly. The Qur'an has therefore given a very accurate description of the Sun not through the use of scientific terms, concepts, and theories, but rather through the analogy of *sirāj wahhājj* that the ordinary human mind can understand.

In the present context of our attempt to understand the nature of light coming from a *miṣbāḥ*, the Light Verse seems to provide a very important clue. The verse reads:

> "God is the Light (*nūr*) of the heavens and the earth. The parable of His Light is as if there were a niche (*mishkāt*) and within it a lamp (*miṣbāḥ*): the lamp enclosed in a glass (*zujājah*): the glass as it were a brilliant star (*kawkab durriy*). Lit from a blessed Tree, an Olive, neither of the East nor of the West, whose oil is well-nigh luminous, though fire scarce touched it: Light upon Light! God does guide whom He will to His Light: God does set forth parables for men: and God knows all things."[97]

The Light Verse is perhaps one verse that received the largest number of special commentaries in the history of Qur'anic exegesis. It has been commented upon from various points of view, including the cosmological and the psychological.[98] Classical exegetes generally interpret the word

---

97. *The Qur'an*, chapter 24 ("The Light"), verse 35.

98. Many well-known Muslim theologians, philosophers, and Sufis wrote commentaries on this verse. Ibn Sīnā, for example, commented upon it from the perspective of faculty psychology. For an English translation of the

*miṣbāḥ* in the above verse to men *sirāj*,[99] since it refers to a self-burning lamp consuming its own fuel to light itself. When this meaning of *miṣbāḥ* is applied to the light-emitting objects adorning the heavens, we have to conclude that the word *maṣābīḥ* in verse 41:12 and verse 67:5 must be signifying the stars. A heaven adorned with the stars could not be our solar system, since the Sun is its only star. It has to be the firmament of the fixed stars that is beyond our solar system but still visible to the naked eye. In the above parable of the Light Verse, the word *kawkab* is used to describe the brilliantly shining glass that results from the burning lamp it encloses, thereby transmitting light in all directions to its furthest reaches. The shining glass (*zujājah*) is likened to a *kawkab durriy* ("brilliant star"). It is clear from the parable that although the glass receives light from the burning lamp, its shining quality is such that it looks like a true star. The Qur'an is thus using the word *kawkab* in this verse to mean a star that is self-luminous rather than a "planet". In consistency with this meaning, we are interpreting the word *kawākib* in verse 37:6-7 to mean "the stars."

With both the words *kawākib* and *maṣābīḥ* in the three verses on the lower heavens (*al-samā' al-dunyā*) having the same meaning of "the stars," we may then infer that by the

---

commentary, see Seyyed Hossein Nasr, *Science and Civilization in Islam* (Cambridge: The Islamic Texts Society, 1987 edition), p. 96. Al-Ghazzālī wrote a commentary on the verse and the Prophetic hadith on the "seventy thousand veils of light and darkness," which he titled *Mishkāt al-anwār* ("The Niche of Lights"). See Al-Ghazzālī, *Mishkāt al-anwār*, trans. W. H. T. Gairdner (Lahore: Sh. Muhammad Ashraf, 1952).

99. Edward W. Lane, *Arabic-English Lexicon*, vol. 2, p. 1643.

phrase *al-samā' al-dunyā* the Qur'an means the firmament of the constellations (*al-burūj*) visible to the naked eye and, naturally also, the firmaments that lie below it, namely our solar system. A point to note is that even if we were to interpret the word *kawkab* in the Light verse as a "planet" our conclusion about the identity of the lower heavens need not have to change, since we have already affirmed *al-samā' al-dunyā* adorned by the *maṣābīḥ* as signifying the heaven of the stars.

In the light of the above understanding of the Qur'anic idea of the lower heavens (*al-samā' al-dunyā*), we may assert that the idea is dictated more by physical than symbolic considerations. Nearness of the heavens is defined in this case in physical terms. The Qur'an equates the lower heavens with the whole cosmic region that is visible to our naked eye. Quite clearly, this physical idea of the lower heavens could not be fitted or integrated into the astronomical models of the cosmos adopted by the classical Muslim astronomers that provide a place and role for planetary and stellar symbols. In making this statement, we do not mean that the classical Muslim astronomical models of the cosmos have become obsolete or irrelevant. These models will still serve a purpose as long as we understand the planetary and stellar symbolism inherent in them. However, our new understanding of the qur'anic idea of the lower heavens (*al-samā' al-dunyā*) in the light of rapid advancement of astronomical knowledge in modern times concerning the cosmic region beyond our solar system calls for the construction of new astronomical models of the cosmos but that still conform to the cosmological teachings of the Qur'an.

Our long discussion of the Qur'anic astronomical picture of the physical cosmos clearly shows the prominent space given by the Qur'an to the issue of the structure of the heavens and the configuration of the celestial bodies in the observable cosmos not only in our solar system but also in other parts of the Milky Way galaxy. It also shows the importance the Qur'an accords to the relationship between the planet earth and the rest of the cosmos. But we need to look at another aspect of the astronomical picture of the solar system that has not yet been depicted. This aspect pertains to the respective motions of the celestial bodies in space, their functions, and their impacts on the planet Earth. The issue of motions of these bodies, especially of the Sun and the Moon is closely related to the vision of the observable cosmos as one vast cosmic clock that serves as a time-measuring system for human benefits.

It is typical of the Qur'an to treat in the same verse the significance of the celestial bodies to human life from various points of view, especially the functional and aesthetic dimensions. Thus, a verse says:

> "It is He Who made the Sun to be a shining glory (*ḍiyā'*) and the Moon to be a light [of beauty] (*nūr*), and measured out stages (*manāzil*) for her; that you know the number of years (*'adad al-sinīn*) and the count [of time] (*al-ḥisāb*). Nowise did God create this but in truth and righteousness. [Thus] does He explain His signs in detail, for those who understand."[100]

This verse is immediately followed by one that refers to the "alternation of the night (*al-layl*) and the day (*al-nahār*)" as among the Signs (*āyāt*) of God.[101] In the above verse, there is first of all a statement about the aesthetic dimension of the

100. *The Qur'an*, chapter 10 ("Jonah"), verse 5.

101. *The Qur'an*, chapter 10 ("Jonah"), verse 6.

creation of the Sun and the Moon, namely the beauty of their respective lights, which are signified by different terms. The use of the term *ḍiyā'* for sunlight and *nūr* for moonlight is to again highlight the fine distinction between the Sun as *sirāj* that radiates its own light and the Moon as *munīr* that reflects light it receives from the Sun. However, both lights have functional roles to play in relation to terrestrial life. Of all the planets in the solar system, our planet Earth has the best location in relation to the Sun. The Earth's ideal distance from the Sun enables it to receive the perfect amount of light and heat for the creation and support of life. The functional role of moonlight in relation to terrestrial life is well-known in traditional Islamic science, especially in the biological sciences.

Then there is the statement about the functional dimension of the creation of the Moon in relation to man's computation of time. God has "measured out *manāzil* ("phases") for her so that man may know the number of years and the count of time." More generally, the Qur'an speaks of the Moon, almost always in conjunction with the Sun,[102] as swimming in space in its own regular orbit. A verse says: "It is He Who created the night and the day, and the Sun and the Moon: all [the celestial bodies] swim along (*yasbaḥūn*), each in its orbit."[103] The Qur'an does not explicitly say that all the planets behave in the same manner in cosmic space as the Sun and the Moon. However, this verse may be interpreted as referring to all celestial bodies

---

102. The word *al-shams* ("The Sun"), occurs 33 times in the Qur'an, while the word *al-qamar* ("The Moon") occurs 27 times. The two bodies are mentioned together 19 times.

103. *The Qur'an*, chapter 21 ("The Prophets"), verse 33.

and not just the Sun and the Moon.[104] The sentence also means that all the celestial bodies share the same type of motion, which the Qur'an indicates with its use of the verb *yasbaḥūn* ("they swim"). We will discuss later the scientific meaning and significance of this celestial "swimming" (*sibāḥa*).

As to the regularity, uniformity and predictability of the respective orbits of the Sun and the Moon, the following verse asserts: "And He has subjected (*sakhkhara*) to you the Sun and the Moon, both diligently (*dā'ibayn*) pursuing their courses ..."[105]The statement "He has subjected to you the Sun and the Moon"[106] in this verse means that God has commanded the two celestial entities to serve man in accordance with his needs and His laws. Being the perfect obedient Muslims that they are, the Sun and the Moon submit themselves to God's Will by diligently and tirelessly observing the laws that He has prescribed for them.

So God uses the word *dā'ibayn* to describe both bodies as diligently and strictly observing His laws governing their courses. The word could not be more fitting, since its active participle *dā'ib* conveys the meaning of being "diligent,

---

104. Yusuf 'Ali renders the statement *kull fī falakin yasbaḥūn* as "all [the celestial bodies] swim along, each in its rounded course." See his *The Meaning of the Holy Qur'an*, p. 663 and p. 939. We have adopted this rendering except that instead of using the phrase "rounded course" we use "orbit."

105. *The Qur'an*, chapter 14 ("Abraham"), verse 33.

106. Compare this statement with the following verse, chapter 7 ("The Heights"), verse 54: "He created the Sun, the Moon, and the stars (*al-nujūm*), all governed by laws under His command (*musakhkharāt bi-amrih*)."

devoted, tireless, persistent, untiring, and indefatigable."[107] Clearly implied in these meanings are features of regularity, uniformity, and predictability that are usually attributed to phenomena governed by exact mathematical laws. Science has confirmed the exact nature of the laws regulating the paths the two bodies traverse in space. From the perspective of the Divine Cosmic Plan, the ideal form of the traversed paths for these celestial bodies for the purpose of meeting human needs for time measurement and calculation would be orbital motions. Thus, in saying that "both the Sun and the Moon diligently pursuing their courses," God is sending the message to man that he can derive the necessary knowledge from their mathematical behaviors for the purpose of time calculation. Some other verses affirm the interpretation that when God created the Sun and the Moon He endowed them with such mathematical properties and behaviors. In one verse, the Qur'an says that God has made "the Sun and the Moon for the reckoning [of time] (*ḥusbān*)."[108]Another verse says: "The Sun and the Moon follow courses [exactly] computed (*bi-ḥusbān*)."[109]

The moon moves in orbit round the Earth, always showing

---

107. See also Maurice Bucaille's discussion of this word as applied to the verse 14:33 in his *The Bible, The Qur'an, and Science*, p. 153.

108. *The Qur'an*, chapter 6 ("The Cattle"), verse 96. The whole verse is actually loaded with meanings related to man's consciousness of passages of time: "He it is that cleaves the day-break [from the dark]; He makes the night for rest and tranquility, and the Sun and the Moon for the reckoning [of time]; such is the Plan and the Design (*taqdīr*) of the Exalted in Might (*al-'Azīz*) and the All-Knowing (*al-'Alīm*)."

109. *The Qur'an*, chapter 55 ("The Most Gracious"), verse 5.

only one side. It does so in an elliptical orbit in the same way the Earth orbits round the Sun. As for the Moon's orbital motion, God has "measured out stages (*manāzil*) for her" (10:6). A related verse says: "And the Moon – We have measured for her mansions (*manāzil*) [to traverse] till she returns like the old [and withered] lower part of a date-stalk."[110] The moon runs through all its phases or stages, increasing and then decreasing, until it disappears but only to appear again looking like a sickle or the old, dried-up lower part of a date-stalk (*al-'urjūn al-qadīm*). The Moon's most visible phases to the naked eye are when it appears as a crescent, a half moon, a three-quarter or gibbous moon, and a full moon. The Moon's orbital motion round the Earth has furnished man with the time concept of "lunar month" to serve as a unit of time measurement for long quantitative periods. The lunar month is the time taken by the Moon to complete its orbit round the Earth. At the more detailed level dealt with by science, however, a fine distinction is made between the orbital period of the Moon around the Earth relative to the Sun, which is called "the synodic month" and its orbital period around the Earth relative to the fixed stars, which is called "the sidereal month."[111]

The Qur'an's reference to the creation of the Moon for the purpose of time measurement serves as the scriptural basis for the Muslim adoption of the lunar calendar not only in the observation of religious rites but also in the conduct of societal

---

110. *The Qur'an*, chapter 36 ("Yā Sīn"), verse 39.

111. The sidereal month is equal to 27.32 days, while the synodic month equals 29.53 days. The most familiar lunar cycle is the synodic month because it governs the well-known cycle of the Moon's phases.

life in all its dimensions as displayed in traditional Islamic civilization. The full significance of the new moon for human life is spelt out in this verse: "They ask you concerning the new moons (*al-ahillah*). Say: they are but signs to mark fixed periods of time (*mawaqīt*) in [the affairs of] men, and for pilgrimage."[112] Quite clearly, in Islam practical religious needs and obligations as dictated by Islamic Divine Law (*al-Sharī'ah*) supplemented the scientific interest inspired by the above astronomical picture of the cosmos to make astronomy a major concern of Muslim scientists. The performance of major religious rights such as the obligatory five daily prayers, fasting in the month of Ramadan, and the pilgrimage to Mecca, all of which require time calculations and time keeping, motivated the Muslims to develop scientific knowledge and technical know-how in mathematical astronomy and related branches of mathematics.

On the basis of the Qur'anic data gathered thus far on the motion of the Sun, it is possible to maintain that, like the Moon, the Sun moves in the cosmic space pursuing a uniform, regular orbital path. It moves with constant speed, and its orbital motion is such that it is possible to calculate the time it takes to complete the orbit. The Qur'an leaves it to science to obtain the detailed mathematical information about these various aspects of the Sun's motion. Its description of the Sun, the Moon, and the planets as "swimming" in their respective orbits is, however, very instructive, but modern exegetes generally tend to avoid rendering *yasbaḥūn* as "they swim," perhaps because they think the idea of celestial bodies swimming in space does not make much sense. Asad prefers to

112. *The Qur'an*, chapter 2 ("The Cow"), verse 189.

adopt the meaning of "to float," which is another meaning of *sabaḥa*, the root verb of *yasbaḥūn*. So he renders the statement *kull fī falakin yasbaḥūn* as "all of them floating through space!"[113] Maurice Bucaille renders it as "each one is travelling in an orbit with its own motion,"[114] because he prefers to have its unambiguous scientific meaning. As earlier mentioned, Yusuf 'Ali renders the statement as "all [the celestial bodies] swim along, each in its rounded course." He prefers this rendering, because he likes the "metaphor of swimming" being applied to the heavenly bodies moving space through space.[115]

In our view, the literary, scientific, and aesthetic significance of the above portion of the verse would be best captured by the idea of "swimming" for several reasons. *First*, it would be an intellectual and scientific landmark in the history of human thought to have the idea of earthly living forms swimming in water extended to the heavenly bodies moving in the ocean of cosmic space in a distinctive way, without compromising the scientific content of the verse or the semantic field of the verb *yasbaḥūn*. *Second*, the idea of swimming as a special kind of physical motion comprehends the idea of floating and the idea of self-propelled motion. Floating, whether in water or in cosmic space, is an aspect of the art of swimming. Similarly, the idea of self-propelled motion is just one of the features of swimming, albeit a core one. To reduce "swimming" to its floating dimension or its self-propelled nature would be to deprive it of both its artistic

113. Muhammad Asad, *The Message of the Qur'an*, p. 588 and p. 808.

114. Maurice Bucaille, *The Bible, The Qur'an and Science*, p. 158-159.

115. 'Abdullah Yusuf 'Ali, *The Meaning of the Holy Qur'an*, note 2695, p. 663.

elements and its theological significance as one of the Signs (*āyāt*) of God. And *third*, in maintaining the idea of swimming, we are called upon to explain why of all kinds of swimming the one performed by the Sun, the Moon, and the planets is the most unique and outstanding. The role of science and mathematics is crucial in helping us in this explanation.

There are several major features of the swimming in space done by the celestial bodies that make it nothing less than miraculous. *First*, each celestial body swims in an almost circular orbit. *Second*, while moving in a "circle" it rotates about its own axis.[116] *Third*, it moves with constant speed so that its orbital period is precise and predictable. The Sun is said to circle the center of the Milky Way galaxy at the speed of about 486,000 miles per hour.[117] Its orbital period is about 230 million years. And *fourth*, this "orbital swim" repeats itself indefinitely in a very exact manner. In our understanding, the Qur'an of course knows the characteristic features of the

---

116. In the case of the Sun, different parts of it rotate at different velocities due to its gaseous composition. Its equator is said to take 25 Earth days to completely rotate.

117. This is equivalent to 135 miles per second or 217 km per second. There are different measurements of the speed, which yield different values. The maximum value recorded is about 250 km per second. It seems that some past Muslim thinkers were aware of the fast speed of the Sun. Al-Ghazzālī, for example, referred to a conversation between the Prophet Muḥammad (May God's salutation and peace be upon him!) and Gabriel (peace be upon him!) concerning the motion of the Sun. The Prophet said to Gabriel: "Has the Sun moved?" Gabriel answered: "No - Yes." The Prophet asked: How so?" Gabriel replied: "Between my saying No and Yes it has moved a distance equal to 500 years." See Al-Ghazzālī, *Mishkāt al-anwār,* p. 89. Al-Ghazzālī also described the Stars as moving every instant through distances of many miles.

motions of the Sun and the Moon, but chose to describe them by using the metaphor of swimming instead of the exact scientific or mathematical language. Now that we know through science that the celestial bodies are characterized by these at once rotational and orbital motions, we could well say that the Qur'an is using the word *yasbaḥūn* ("swimming") in reference to their motions precisely with the view of alluding them to their features indicated above. With all these established features, the swimming of these celestial bodies could only be described as knowledge-laden, of artistic beauty, and inimitable!

We encounter several other Qur'anic descriptions of the motions of the Sun and the Moon that deserve our treatment. We need to establish whether these descriptions only appear to be different from the descriptions already discussed in the terminological sense or they offer new scientific data about the motions of these celestial bodies. The first of these descriptions is in the statement *yajrī li-ajalin musamman* as contained in this verse: "He has subjected the Sun and the Moon [to His Law]; each one runs [its course] for a term appointed (*yajrī li-ajalin musamman*). He regulates all affairs, explaining the Signs in detail so that you may believe with certainty in the meeting with your Lord."[118] The second description is in the statement *wa'l-shams tajrī li-mustaqarr lahā* as contained in this verse: "And the Sun runs his course for a period determined for him (*wa'l-shams tajrī li-mustaqarr lahā*): that is the decree of [Him], the Exalted in Might, the All-Knowing."[119]The third description *la'l-shams yanbaghī lahā an tudrik al-qamar* is in

118. *The Qur'an*, chapter 13 ("The Thunder"), verse 2.

119. *The Qur'an*, chapter 36 ("Yā Sīn"), verse 38.

the following verse: "It is not permitted to the Sun to catch up the Moon (*la'l-shams yanbaghī lahā an tudrik al-qamar*), nor can the Night outstrip the Day: each [just] swims along in [its own] orbit [according to Law]."[120] And the fourth description is in this verse: "... when is the Day of Resurrection (*yawm al-qiyāmah*)? ... when the Moon is buried in darkness, and the Sun and the Moon are joined together (*jumi'a al-shams wa'l-qamar*) ..."[121]

All the above four descriptions about the Sun and the Moon appear to be about "new" aspects of their orbital motions. In the first description *kullun yajrī li-ajalin musamman*[122] the "new things" about the motion of the Sun and the Moon are the use of the verb *yajrī* and the phrase *ajalin musamman*. We maintain that the whole description may be rendered as "each [celestial body] orbits in a fixed period." Verse 21:33 has already clearly established the orbital motion of the celestial bodies. Although not all of the meanings conveyed by the root verb *jarā* from which *yajrī* is derived, imply "orbital motion," one of them does. This particular root meaning is "to circulate." But "to circulate" means to move in a circle starting from a point of origin and coming back to it. What we call "orbital motion" in astronomy is precisely of this kind. Given the fact that the motion of the Sun is necessarily orbital in nature, it is this particular meaning of *jarā* that we should adopt. It is thus appropriate to interpret *kullun yajrī* as meaning "each [body] orbits or revolves." Once the idea of

120. *The Qur'an*, chapter 36 ("Yā Sīn"), verse 40.

121. *The Qur'an*, chapter 75 ("The Resurrection"), verses 6-9.

122. This statement is found in three other verses: 31:29; 35:13; 39:5.

orbital motion is established, the interpretation of *li-ajalin musamman* as meaning "in a pre-determined, fixed or designated period" follows suit. There is a kind of "absolute deadline" that the orbiting or revolving body has to be back exactly at the point of "origin" of the orbit. This fixed or pre-determined period is precisely the time taken by the celestial body in question to complete its orbit. The description *kullun yajrī li-ajalin musamman* in verse 13:2 thus provides the scriptural basis for the idea of each of the Sun, the Moon and other celestial bodies having a fixed orbital period.

Verse 13:2 complemented with verse 21:33 furnishes us with the theological-metaphysical significance of the orbital motions of the celestial bodies, in particular the Sun and the Moon. Three points of significance are mentioned in the concluding statements in the verse. *First*, God regulates all affairs (*yudabbir al-amr*), meaning that the orbital motion of the Sun and other celestial bodies is determined by Him in accordance with His Laws. *Second*, He explains His Signs in detail (*yufaṣṣil al-āyāt*). In the Qur'an, generally speaking, "His Signs" refer to His Names and Qualities that are disclosed or manifested through His creation. We see that different aspects of creation point to different sets of Attributes and Qualities that are predominantly manifested. In the case of the creation of the solar system, the list of the associated Names and Qualities that have been mentioned in the Qur'an includes the Omniscient (*al-'Alīm*), the Planner-Designer-Creator (*al-Khāliq*), the Exalted in Might (*al-'Azīz*), the Wise (*al-Ḥakīm*), and the All-Powerful (*al-Qadīr*). And *third*, the detailed explanation of God's Signs as displayed in the orbital motion of the Sun and the Moon is so that man may "believe with certainty in the meeting" with his Lord (*bi-liqā' rabbikum tūqinūn*). The idea of a return to the origin in the orbital motion of celestial bodies is a good reminder of man's return to his origin to meet his Lord. Moreover, it is a constant reminder since the orbits repeat themselves without fail.

In the second description *wa'l-shams tajrī li-mustaqarr lahā*, the "new thing" about the motion of the Sun is the phrase *tajrī li-mustaqarr lahā*. As in the first description, we may render *tajrī* as "the Sun orbits." As for the phrase *li-mustaqarr lahā*, we have to admit that it is not an easy one to interpret. It allows for various interpretations. So we find different interpretations among the classical exegetes just as we also find among their modern counterparts. Fakhr al-Dīn Rāzī interprets the phrase as meaning "to its point of rest," which he explains as "to the time of daily sunset." This interpretation is symbolically admissible, but it is not helpful to our attempt to understand its scientific meaning. From the scientific point of view, the position attributed to 'Abdullāh ibn Mas'ūd, the Prophet's companion noted for his deep knowledge of Qur'anic exegesis, that *li-mustaqarr lahā* should be read *lā mustaqarr lahā*[123] would be of greater significance. The latter reading of the phrase would give the meaning of "without having any rest." In other words, the Sun moves on unceasingly. Ibn 'Abbās interprets *li-mustaqarr lahā* as meaning "to its mansion" and he adds "the sun runs in the day and at night without any resting place."[124] Yusuf 'Ali renders it as "for a period determined for him."[125] Asad simply renders it as "in an

123. See Muhammad Asad, *The Message of the Qur'an*, p. 807-808.

124. See *Tafsīr ibn 'Abbās*, p. 500.

125. 'Abdullah Yusuf 'Ali, *The Meaning of the Holy Qur'an*, p. 939. Yusuf 'Ali offers his interpretation on the basis of the Qur'anic usage of the word

orbit of its own."[126] Bucaille translates it as "to a settled place."[127] Regarding this "settled place," he is of the view that "modern astronomy has been able to locate it exactly and has even given it a name, the Solar Apex."[128] As he explains it, "the solar system is evolving in space toward a point situated in the Constellation of Hercules (*alpha lyrae*) whose exact location is firmly established." Bucaille adds, the solar system is moving toward the "settled place" at the known speed of about 12 miles per second.

The three senses of *mustaqarr* indicated by Yusuf 'Ali may serve as a useful guide in our rendering of the descriptive phrase *tajrī li-mustaqarr lahā*. The important thing to note is that the description is about the orbital motion of the Sun, which modern astronomy is able to know much more than what classical astronomy could tell us. The orbit of the Sun is basically the orbit of the whole solar system around the center of the Milky Way galaxy of which it is a part. It seems that the various commentators mentioned above are stating the correct and relevant things about the orbital motion of the Sun, but each of these renderings pertains to just some aspects of this

---

*mustaqarr*. He points out that the Qur'an uses the word in three senses. The first sense is that of "a limit of time, a period determined" as in verse 6:67: "For every Message is a limit of time (*mustaqarr*), and soon shall you know it." The second sense is that of "a place of rest" and the third sense that of "a dwelling place" as in verse 2:36: "On earth will be your dwelling place and your means of livelihood for a time." He considers the first sense as the best applicable to the phrase *li-mustaqarr lahā*.

126. Muhammad Asad, *The Message of the Qur'an*, p. 807.

127. Maurice Bucaille, *The Bible, The Qur'an, and Science*, p. 165.

128. Maurice Bucaille, *The Bible, The Qur'an, and Science*, p. 166.

motion and not its whole picture as is perhaps attended by the word *mustaqarr*. Given the cosmic significance of the Sun's orbital motion, we are persuaded to interpret *mustaqarr* in the above phrase as conveying both the ideas of "fixed and limited periods" and "destination." The assertion "that is the decree of [Him], the Exalted in Might (*al-'Azīz*), the All-Knowing (*al-'Alīm*)" that comes immediately after the statement *tajrī li-mustaqarr lahā* seems to suggest that it is alluding to more profound cosmic realities than what we presently know.

The orbital period of the Sun and its planetary system is pre-determined and fixed, for which reason science is able to calculate it. The orbital motion is of limited period in the sense that we will reach a point in time when the solar system will collapse as necessitated by the eschatological event of *yawm al-qiyāmah* ("The Resurrection") that is indicated in the fourth description of the Sun's motion "when the Sun and the Moon are joined together" (*jumi'a al-shams wa'l-qamar*). This eschatological joining together of the Sun and the Moon is important to be borne in mind when we seek to obtain a more enlightened understanding of the meaning of *li-mutaqarr lahā* in reference to the Sun's motion. While orbiting around the center of our galaxy, the solar system is also journeying to an "unknown place." So the idea of a "settled place" as discussed by Bucaille cannot be simply dismissed. But the Qur'an reminds us that one day, which God alone knows, "the Sun and the Moon" that are now beautifully kept apart by certain physical forces and laws "will be joined together" (75:9).

In the third description *lā al-shams yanbaghī lahā an tudrik al-qamar*, the "new thing" about the motion of the Sun is the idea of law and order that prevails in the solar system. But this idea is closely related to the orbital motion of the Sun. It is because each celestial body swims in its own orbit, that is, it rotates and revolves according to well-defined laws that the Sun and the Moon will never catch up each other. Similarly, it is because of the same fact that Night and Day follow each other in a harmonious way. Commenting on the above Qur'anic description, Ibn 'Abbās maintains that "it is not proper for the Sun to rise where the Moon appears such that it takes away its light" just as "the night does not come at the time of the day such that it eclipses its brightness."[129]

129. *Tafsīr ibn 'Abbās,* p. 500.

*Chapter Four*

# The Architectural Picture of the Universe

Architecture is about the design and construction of buildings, bridges and other constructed works that require a similar kind of knowledge and expertise. It has also an aesthetic dimension. Many verses of the Qur'an present the cosmos as an architectural work that is divinely planned, designed, and constructed. There is a whole set of vocabulary in the Qur'an pertaining to the divine architectural work. However, the focus of God's architectural concern is with the idea of the Earth as man's planetary home, thereby illustrating the centrality of man in His scheme of creation. The construction of the rest of the cosmos is envisaged in the light of its functional role in relation to the fulfillment of the Earth's needs. Viewed as a whole, the cosmos is seen as an edifice with a solid construction, a perfect architectural design, and beautiful ornamentation.

Since the architectural and astronomical pictures of the cosmos are closely connected to each other on a good number of issues, some of the verses cited in the discussion on the astronomical picture will feature again in this section but with an emphasis on their architectural significance. The core words in the Qur'anic vocabulary in architecture are derived from the root verb *banā*, which convey the meanings of "to build, erect, and construct something." The words derived from the root verb of the first form, *banā*, occur 11 times in the Qur'an in their verbal forms and also 11 times in their noun forms. But in only 7 of these occurrences we have explicit references to the construction of the heavens. We cite below the most relevant verses to cosmic architecture.

> "[He] Who has made the Earth your couch and the heavens (*al-samā'*) your canopy (*binā'*) ..." (2:22).

> "Do they not look at the sky (*al-samā'*) above them? – how We have constructed it (*banaynāha*) and adorned (*zayyannā*) it, and there are no flaws in it?"[130] ʿ

> "It is God Who has made for you the Earth as a resting place (*qarāra*), and the sky (*al-samā'*) as a canopy (*binā'*)..."[131]

> "With power and skill did We construct (*banaynā*) the heavens: for it is We Who create the vastness of space" (51:47).

> "And [have We not] built (*banaynā*) over you the seven firmaments, and placed [therein] a light of splendor?" (78:12-13).

> "He Who created the seven heavens (*sabʿ samāwāt*) one above another: no want of proportion will you see in the creation of [God] Most Gracious" (67:3).

> "God is He Who raised the heavens without any pillars (*bi-ghayr ʿamad*) that you can see; and is established on

---

130. *The Qur'an*, chapter 50 ("Qāf"), verse 6.

131. *The Qur'an*, chapter 40 ("The Forgiver"), verse 64.

the Throne [of Authority]"[132]

"And We have made the heavens as a canopy well guarded (*saqfan maḥfūẓan*)".[133]

"What! Are you the more difficult to create or the heaven (*al-samā'*)? God has constructed (*banā*) it: on high has He raised its canopy (*samk*), and He has given it order and perfection (*sawwāha*)."[134]

"By the firmament and its [wonderful] structure (*mā banāha*)."[135]

It is clear from these verses and the various previously discussed verses on the Earth as a spread out in its various aspects that God has provided a planetary home for man. This planetary home has a solid, fully functional, and spacious "floor" and a multi-layered "roof" or canopy that is perfectly designed and skillfully constructed as well as a beautifully adorned ceiling. The raising of the heavens without any pillars visible to us, right up to the Throne (13:2), deserves a discussion, albeit briefly, because of its scientific significance. There is a need to explain, from the scientific point of view, what is it that keeps the various heavy layers of the firmament and the celestial bodies placed in them in firm place and prevents them from "collapsing." Science presents gravity as the key explanatory factor for the stability of the heavens.

---

132. *The Qur'an*, chapter 13 ("The Thunder"), verse 2. See the only other similar verse, chapter 31 ("Luqmān"), verse 10.

133. *The Qur'an*, chapter 21 ("The Prophets"), verse 32.

134. *The Qur'an*, chapter 79 ("Those Who Tear Out"), verses 27-28.

135. *The Qur'an*, chapter 91 ("The Sun"), verse 5.

Gravity is defined as the natural force of attraction between any two massive bodies. Since the attracting force of a body is directly proportional to its mass, the more massive body tends to attract to its center the smaller ones. In the solar system, it is the sheer size of the Sun[136] that gives it the gravity needed to hold the system together for it accounts for more than 99.8% of all the mass in the system. The Sun's gravitational pull exerted on the planets keep them in their orbits instead of flying off into space. At the wider cosmic level, our solar system itself revolves around the center of the Milky Way galaxy, which shows very high gravitational attraction.

The Qur'an maintains that the stability of the heavenly roofs or canopies is not a permanent cosmic feature. It is God's Will that keeps them from collapsing. But by God's Will, when the eschatological event of the Resurrection Day (*yawm al-qiyāmah*) comes, the whole cosmic system will collapse.

The architectural picture of the cosmos is also about the adornment of its heavens. Two of the verses mentioned above pertain to this adornment (50:6 and 78:13). There are more verses about it as indicated by the occurrence of the word *zayyana*, the root verb of the second form and the noun *zīnah*. The word *zayyana*, which conveys the root meaning of "to adorn, decorate, ornament, and embellish," occurs 26 times in the Qur'an, while its noun form, occurs 19 times. However, in only 8 of these occurrences are references specifically made mostly to the heavens and one or two to the Earth. These verses are cited below:

> "It is We Who have positioned constellations (*burūj*) in the firmament (*al-samā'*) and endowed them with

136. The Sun is said to be 333,000 times more massive than the Earth.

beauty for all to behold (*zayyannāhā li'l-nāẓirīn*)"(15:16).

"We have indeed adorned (*zayyannā*) the lower heavens (*al-samā' al-dunyā*) with the beauty of the stars (*zīnat al-kawākib*)..."(37:6).

"And We have adorned (*zayyannāhā*) the lower heavens (*al-samā' al-dunyā*) with lamps (*maṣābīḥ*)...."[137]

"Do they not look at the sky (*al-samā'*) above them? – how We have made it and adorned (*zayyannah*)....?" (50:6)

"That which is on earth We have made but as a glittering show for the earth...."[138]

There are verses pertaining to the adornment or the beautification of the heavens but without being signified by the word *zayyana* or *zīnah*. A good example is this verse: "Blessed is He Who made constellations (*burūj*) in the skies (*al-samā'*), and placed therein a Lamp (*sirājan*) [*i.e.* the Sun] and a light-giving Moon (*qamaran munīran*)" (25:61). Another is the following: "And We placed a lamp full of blazing splendor (*sirājan wahhājjan*)" (78:13). The important thing to be observed with regard to the architectural picture is that regardless of the descriptive word used to signify the aesthetic dimension of the cosmos as an architectural work, its predominant element that captures the human imagination is celestial light objects in varying forms.

---

137. See verse 12, chapter 41 ("The Expounded") and verse 5, chapter 67, which are almost similar in their wordings.

138. *The Qur'an*, chapter 18 ("The Cave"), verse 7.

*Chapter Five*

# The Picture of the Cosmos as a Divine Kingdom

This picture depicts the cosmos as one vast territory ruled by God Who has at His Command innumerable cosmic agents and forces (*junūd*).[139] One dimension of this picture pertains to the causal relations that exist between the different parts and forces of the cosmos. These causal relations are governed by God's laws, to which science refers as "natural laws," that while depicting God as the Ultimate Cause also recognizes the role of creatures, especially the angels, as secondary causes. The cosmos as a divine kingdom extends from the Divine Throne (*al-'arsh*) to the furthest region of the

139. The Qur'an speaks of the forces of the heavens and the earth (*junūd al-samāwāt wa'l-arḍ*) belonging to God. See verses 48:4 and 48:7. Exegetes generally, including Ibn 'Abbās, interpret the word *junūd* in these two verses to signify the angels. See *Tafsīr ibn 'Abbās*, p. 596. The angels are the invisible creatures of God that serve as intermediaries between Him and the physical world, faithfully carrying out His command to administer the cosmos and serve mankind. For a detailed treatment of the nature, classification, and cosmic functions of the angels in the English language, see Sachiko Murata, 'Angels,' Seyyed Hossein Nasr, ed., *Islamic Spirituality: Foundations* (New York: Crossroad, 1987), pp. 324-344; also Sachiko Murata and William C. Chittick, *The Vision of Islam*, pp. 84-92.

material world where the Earth is located. The Qur'an says: "He rules [all] affairs (*yudabbiru al-amr*) from the heavens to the Earth."[140] Equivalently, it says: "God is He Who created seven firmaments and of the earth a similar number. Through the midst of them [all] descends His command (*al-amr*): that you may know that God has power over all things, and that God comprehends all things in [His] Knowledge."[141] These verses mean that we should not entertain even for a single moment the idea that there is a part of the cosmos that exists independently of God's Laws and sovereignty. So *yudabbir al-amr* is an important qur'anic phrase signifying the divine governance of cosmic affairs. These cosmic affairs will come to an end, but we do not know when this future event will happen. The same verse continues: "in the end will [all affairs] go up to Him, on a Day, the space whereof will be [as] a thousand years of your reckoning."

The word *'arsh*, including in its plural form *'urūsh*, is mentioned 29 times in the Qur'an. It is in only 21 of these occurrences that the word refers to the Divine Throne. When thrice it occurs in the plural, it is signifying the meaning of "roofs" of buildings (2:259) and trellises used in vineyards (18:42). Four times it is referring to the throne of Queen Balqis, who was invited by the Prophet Solomon (peace be upon him!) and subsequently submitted to his religion of Islam.[142] And once it signifies the symbolic throne of dignity on which the Prophet Joseph (peace be upon him!) has raised his parents

140. *The Qur'an*, chapter 32 ("The Prostration"), verse 5.

141. *The Qur'an*, chapter 65 ("Divorce"), verse 12.

142. For the Qur'anic passages referring to the throne of Balqis, see *The Qur'an*, chapter 27 ("The Ants"), verses 23 and 38-42.

(12:100). When the word *'arsh* refers most of the times to the Divine Throne, it mainly conveys the idea of God as firmly established on the throne of authority with His ownership, power, and governance embracing the whole cosmos. The Qur'anic expression for "being established on the throne of authority" is *istawā 'alā'l-'arsh*. An example is this verse: "[God] the Most Gracious (*al-Raḥmān*) is firmly established on the throne [of authority]."[143] The idea of an all-embracing ownership, dominion, and lordship is expressed through several expressions, especially *lahu mā fi'l-samāwāt wa'l-arḍ* ("to Him belongs what is in the heavens and the Earth") and *lahu mulk al-samāwat wa'l-arḍ* ("to Him belongs the dominion of the heavens and the Earth"). A verse says: "To Him belongs what is in the heavens and the Earth, and all between them, and all beneath the soil."[144] Another verse says: "He to whom belongs the dominion (*mulk*) of the heavens and the Earth."[145]

For some Muslim cosmologists and astronomers, the Throne (*al-'arsh*) also symbolizes the starless ninth heaven, which is the highest. For Sufi cosmologists such as Ibn al-'Arabī, it symbolizes the *barzakh* ("isthmus") between God and creation.[146] As a *barzakh* the Throne is neither divine nor

---

143. *The Qur'an*, chapter 20 ("Ṭā Ḥā"), verse 5. The expression *istawā 'alā'l-'arsh* occurs in six other verses: 7:54; 10:3; 13:2; 25:59; 32:4; 57:4.

144. *The Qur'an*, chapter 20 ("Ṭā Ḥā "), verse 6. The phrase *li'Llāh* [or *lahu*] *mā fi'l-samāwāt wa'l-arḍ* occurs 39 times in the Qur'an.

145. *The Qur'an*, chapter 25 ("The Criterion"), verse 2. The phrase *lahu mulk al-samāwāt wa'l-arḍ* occurs 20 times in the Qur'an.

146. Ibn al-'Arabī calls this *barzakh* the highest *barzakh*, because it is to be distinguished from the lower kinds of *barzakh*, for example, the *barzakh* between the "life of this world" and the "last world" where souls after death

creaturely. The phrase *Rabb al-'arsh* ("Lord of the Throne"), which occurs six times in the Qur'an,[147] means that the Throne is not divine. According to Ibn al-'Arabī, "it is the first bodily thing that assumes a specific shape."[148] But the Throne upon which the Most Gracious (*al-Raḥmān*) (20:5) sat encompasses the entire manifest cosmos. This means that it is also beyond Creation[149] that is identified with the seven heavens and the Earth. Ikhwān al-Ṣafā', Ibn Sīnā, and Ibn al-'Arabī, all of them place the Pedestal or Footstool (*kursī*) below the Throne (*'arsh*), although it is also a symbol of Divine power and authority. The Qur'an asserts that "God's Footstool embraces (*wasi'a*) the heavens and the earth" (2:255). It is then possible to view the Divine Throne (*al-'arsh*) and the Divine Footstool (*al-kursī*) as the upper and lower ends of the above defined *barzakh* respectively.

The idea of the whole cosmos being subjected to God's Laws is conveyed by such Qur'anic terms as *sakhkhara*, *musakhkharāt*, and *taqdīr*. The word *sakhkhara*, the root verb of the second form, conveys the meaning of to subject, make subservient, submissive, manageable.[150] The word occurs 22

---

have to be till the eschatological event called *ba'th* ("Uprising") happens. See William C. Chittick, *The Self-Disclosure of God*, p. 62.

147. See the verses 9:129; 21:22; 23:86; 23:116; 27:26; 43:82.

148. William C. Chittick, *The Self-Disclosure of God*, p. xxx.

149. That the Throne is beyond the realm of Creation is affirmed in a symbolical manner by the Qur'anic statements that "eight angels will, that Day, bear the Throne of your Lord above them" (69:17) and that the Archangel Gabriel has "power and rank before the Lord of the Throne" (81:20).

150. Edward W. Lane, *Arabic-English Lexicon*, vol. 1, p. 1324.

times in the Qur'an. In all these occurrences except one, the word is used to convey the core message that God has subjected or made subservient parts or the whole of creation to man's use. An example is this verse "Do you not see that God has subjected (*sakhkhara*) to your [use] all things in the heavens and on earth, and has made his bounties flow to you in exceeding measure, [both] seen (*ẓāhirah*) and unseen (*bāṭinah*)?"[151] The sole case in which the word is used otherwise is in reference to the ancient 'Ad people who were destroyed by an exceedingly violent wind that God has made (*sakhkhara*) to rage against them seven nights and eight days successively.[152] In subjecting creation to man's use God does not, however, give him total freedom to use it as he pleases.

There is a universal law of subjection and subservience that is binding on both creation and man. Creation is subjected to man's use through its submission to the Divine Laws. For example, God subjected "the Sun and the Moon" by making each of them "revolving in an orbit for a fixed period" (31:29). The laws governing their motion are Divine Laws in the sight of religion, but science calls them "natural laws." As for man, it is morally incumbent upon him to use whatever "services" rendered by the Sun and the Moon in accordance with the Laws God has revealed to His Prophets. The last Divine Law for humanity has been revealed to Prophet Muḥammad (May God's salutation and peace be upon him!). This means that for humanity in our times and also in the future until the end of the world the ethical teachings governing the use of creation would be best be found in the Qur'an.

---

151. *The Qur'an*, chapter 31 ("Luqmān"), verse 20.

152. *The Qur'an*, chapter 69 ("The Sure Reality"), verse 7.

The idea of subjection and subservience of creation to man's use is also found in the Qur'an through the use of the word *musakhkharat*, the passive participle form of *sakhkhara*. The word occurs three times there. One of the verses is this: "… and the Stars (*al-nujūm*) are in subjection (*musakhkharāt*) by His command (*bi-amrih*)."[153] The word *taqdīr* is also closely related to the idea of laws that have been divinely ordained for the various cosmic phenomena. It has the primary meaning of the determination of a thing according to a measure. We have earlier explained in this chapter that *taqdīr* is the core meaning of *khalaqa* and God is *al-Khāliq* inasmuch as He is a *muqaddir* ("Planner"), a word related to *taqdīr*. The divine determination (*taqdīr*) of things results in their subjection to precise laws.

The word *taqdīr*, the verbal noun form of *qaddara*, which is the root verb of the second form, occurs 5 times in the Qur'an, while the latter occurs 16 times. Verse 6:96 says: "He makes … the Sun and the Moon for the reckoning [of time]: such is the *taqdīr* of the Exalted in Might (*al-'Azīz*) and the All-Knowing (*al-'Alīm*)." God plans and determines for the Sun and the Moon to serve man for the calculation of time. So He subjected them to orbital motions with precise mathematical laws that man can discover and utilize for the purpose of time calculation. We encounter the same idea of Divine determination of measurement but through the use of the word *qaddara*. This word conveys among others the meanings of to predetermine, ordain, decree, measure, assign, and value. An example of the qur'anic use of *qaddara* is this verse: "And the Moon – We have measured (*qaddara*) for it mansions

153. *The Qur'an*, chapter 16 ("The Bee"), verse 12. For the other two verses, see 7:54 and 16:79.

(*manāzil*) to traverse..." (36:39). Another is this: "[He] Who has created, and further, given order and proportion (*sawwā)* and Who has ordained laws (*qaddara*) and gave guidance."[154]

A single verse that best captures most if not all the important ideas pertaining to Divine authority, power and sovereignty, ownership and lordship, and governance and the idea of cosmic law and order is perhaps the following:

> "Your Guardian-Lord (*Rabb*) is God, Who created the heavens and the earth in six days, and is firmly established on the Throne [of authority] (*istawā 'alā'l-'arsh*): He draws the night as a veil over the day, each seeking the other in rapid succession: He created the Sun, the Moon, and the Stars, [all] governed by laws under His command (*musakhkharāt bi-amrihi*). Is it not His all creation (*al-khalq*) and command and governance (*al-amr*)? Blessed be God, the Cherisher and Sustainer of the worlds (*Rabb al-'ālamīn*)."[155]

Another set of qur'anic verses that is important to be considered in our depiction of the cosmos as a divine kingdom characterized by law and order is one in which the noun *qadar* is used to signify this aspect of the cosmic reality. The idea of *qadar* is of special significance to science, since it generally pertains to precise measurement that is more detailed in nature.[156] A very good example to illustrate this idea is this verse about the supply of rain water to the planet Earth: "And

---

154. *The Qur'an*, chapter 87 ("The Most High"), verses 2-3.

155. *The Qur'an*, chapter 7 ("The Heights"), verse 54.

156. The word *qadar* occurs 11 times in the Qur'an: 2:236 (twice); 13:17; 15:21; 20:40; 23:18; 33:38; 42:27; 43:11; 54:49; and 77:22.

[He] Who sends down rain [from time to time] from the sky in due measure (*bi-qadar*) and with it We raise to life (*ansharnā*) a land that is dead (*baldatan maytan*); likewise will you be raised [from the dead]."[157] The general principle of due proportion and measure is contained in this verse: "Verily, We have created everything in due proportion and measure."[158]

157. *The Qur'an*, chapter 40 ("The Gold Adornments"), verse 11.

158. *The Qur'an*, chapter 54 ("The Moon"), verse 49.

*Chapter Six*

# The Universe as a World of Lights and Darkness

One of the Names and Qualities of God is *al-Nūr*, meaning the Absolute Light. He manifests His light in the whole of creation. The Qur'an says: "God is the Light of the heavens and the earth" (24:35). This verse has been cited in full in our discussion of the astronomical picture. God manifests His Light in the universe in such a way that the creatures constitute a hierarchy of lights. God's first creatures were made from pure (spiritual) light. These are the angels, which as earlier mentioned were referred to by Muslim philosopher-scientists as *'uqūl* ("intellects"). After and below the angelic world of light come the creatures of fire, which are intermediate in nature between the spiritual and the physical. The jinn species are described in the Qur'an as "creatures of fire." This non-physical, subtle fire is a grosser form of light.

Ontologically below the world of the creatures of fire is the physical world in which are found many kinds of light-emitting objects. There are the stars in the heavens, including the Sun, that are self-luminous in nature. Then we have celestial objects such as the Moon and the planets that reflect the light which they receive from the Sun. The quoted Light Verse seeks among others to teach man the spiritual lesson that "a polished or transparent object like a glass can shine brilliantly even with light not of its own but from another source."[159] The verse is about the spiritual significance of the phenomenon of reflected light. The purpose of man's existence is to reflect to the best degree the Light of the Divine Names and Qualities so that he will become the "Perfect Man" (*al-insān al-kāmil*).

Some creatures on the planet Earth glow at night with different degrees of light intensity. In accordance with the GSD principle, God as *al-Nūr* ("The Light") manifests or discloses this Quality of His in all creatures, but the presence of light in them is of varying degrees. Classical Islamic light cosmology, which is based on this qur'anic doctrine of "light upon light" (*nūr 'alā nūr*), considers matter as having the least presence of light. It views matter as light in its most coagulated and solidified form. The relationship between matter and light is an issue which modern physics is only beginning to understand through its new branch known as quantum physics. The above discussion of the various creatures in relation to light shows that these creatures are hierarchically ordered in the cosmos in conformity with the degrees of intensity of light manifested in them.

The word *nūr* occurs 43 times in the Qur'an. In 11 of these occurrences it is contrasted with darkness (*ẓulumāt*), but only once the contrasting pair pertains to the macrocosm, the cosmos external to man. The exceptional verse says: "Praise be

159. In the parable of God's Light, the self-luminous object that emits its own light is "the lamp" (*miṣbāḥ*) and the object receiving this light to the point of shining brilliantly, thereby reflecting intensely this light, is the glass enclosing the lamp. This parable offers us with an insight into the various degrees of light both in the macrocosm and in the microcosm.

to God, Who created the heavens and the earth, and made the darkness (*ẓulumāt*) and the light (*nūr*)."[160] In the other 10 occurrences, the contrasting pair pertains to the microcosm, the universe within man. More precisely, the pair signifies the contrasting states of spiritual light and darkness in human souls. The Qur'an seeks to highlight the contrast between light and darkness, because the pair refers to realities in the external cosmos and in the souls of men. There are zones of light and darkness in the external cosmos, a cosmic fact that results from a principle in light cosmology, according to which "a decreasing presence of light is necessarily followed by an increasing darkness." In the physical world itself, the Qur'an refers, for example, to a rain-laden cloud in which are zones of darkness (*ẓulumāt*), thunder, and lightning (*barq*).[161]The zone of light in the cloud is identified with that of lightning, which is very transient in nature and therefore serves as a very instructive similitude for man.

As for the phenomena of light and darkness in human souls, the Qur'an refers 7 times to the availability of Divine guidance to help lead men from the depths of darkness (*ẓulumāt*) into light (*nūr*), that is, a spiritually enlightened state. One of these verses says: "A Messenger, who rehearses to you the Signs of God containing clear explanations that he may lead forth those who believe and do righteous deeds from the depths of darkness into light."[162] Here and in three other verses,[163] the reference is to the souls of the believers. In

160. *The Qur'an*, chapter 6 ("The Cattle"), verse 1.

161. *The Qur'an*, chapter 2 ("The Cow"), verse 19.

162. *The Qur'an*, chapter 65 ("Divorce"), verse 11.

163. The other verses are 2:257; 33:43; 57:9

another verse, the reference is to human souls in general (14:1). There is one verse (14:5) in which the hope is directed at the people of Prophet Moses (peace be upon him!), and another (5:16) at the People of the Book in general.

In one occurrence of the contrasting pair, by way of instruction, the Qur'an poses this question to the human mind: "Are the blind equal with those who see? Or the depths of darkness with light?"[164] The answer of course is very obvious to all right-minded people. The Qur'an seeks to emphasize again that the two could not be alike: "The blind and the seeing are not alike; nor are the depths of darkness and the light."[165] In the only other occurrence of the contrasting pair yet to be considered, the verse in question refers to the rejecters of faith being misled into darkness: "Of those who reject faith (*alladhīna kafarū*) their patrons are the Evil Ones: from light they will lead them forth into the depths of darkness."[166]Interestingly, this is the only verse in the Qur'an that speaks of souls of men being misled into darkness. Moreover, it is not God that misled men, but rather the transgressors against God's Laws and guidance (*al-ṭāghūt*). It is very clear that the preoccupation of the Qur'an is with guiding people from the depths of darkness into light and reminding men of the Evil Ones among them who are bent on misleading them into the depths of darkness.

Even in the 32 occurrences of the word *nūr* where it is not mentioned together with "darkness" (*ẓulumāt*), it is mainly

164. *The Qur'an*, chapter 13 ("The Thunder"), 16.

165. *The Qur'an*, chapter 35 ("The Originator"), verses 19-20.

166. *The Qur'an*, chapter 2 ("The Cow"), verse 257.

used to convey the meaning of light of Divine guidance for man, including in relation to the attempts by the rejecters of faith to extinguish it. In several of its occurrences, the word *nūr* refers to accomplished light in the souls of the believers[167] and the "perfect light" which they desire to have (66:8) as well as to the lack of light in the souls of the unbelievers. One verse deserves to be cited here because its similitude to describe the state of the souls of the unbelievers is drawn from zones of darkness in a deep ocean. The verse says:

> "Or [the unbelievers' state] is like the depths of darkness in a vast deep ocean, overwhelmed with billow topped by billow, topped by [dark] clouds; depths of darkness, one above another (*ẓulumāt ba'ḍuhā fawqa ba'ḍ*); if a man stretches out his hands, he can hardly see it! For any to whom God gives no light, there is no light!"[168]

There are, however, 4 occurrences in which the word *nūr* pertains to the macrocosm. One verse (10:5) refers to *nūr* as the reflected but beautiful light of the Moon as contrasted with the Sun's own light (*ḍiyā'*) that makes it a "shining glory." Sunlight and moonlight represent two grades of light in the physical world. *Nūr* is mentioned twice in the parable of God's Light in the Light Verse (24:35), which may be interpreted both macrocosmically and microcosmically. There is another occurrence (71:16) in which *nūr* again refers to the light of the Moon but this time differentiated from the Sun viewed as a Lamp (*sirāj*) and the significance of both is highlighted in the

167. The Qur'an uses the word *nūrihim* ("their light") to describe this accomplished light. See verses 57:12; 57:19; and 66:8.

168. *The Qur'an*, chapter 24 ("The Light"), verse 40.

context of their being positioned together in the heavens (71:15-16). Verses 10:5 and 71:16 are variations to the same theme of the Sun and the Moon as sources of different grades of light.

Our foregoing discussion on the cosmos as layers of light and darkness makes references to different levels of light and darkness in the souls of men. So just as we may speak of hierarchically ordering light in the macrocosm, we may also speak of hierarchically ordering light and darkness in the microcosm. We have referred to attempts by past Muslim scholars to interpret the Light Verse from the microcosmic perspective of faculty psychology. Al-Ghazzālī interprets the Light Verse together with the above "Darkness verse" (24:40) and the Prophetic hadith on the 70,000 veils of light and darkness. He quoted the hadith as follows:

> God has 70,000 veils of light and darkness: were He to withdraw their curtain, then would the splendors of His Aspect surely consume everyone who apprehended Him with his sight."[169]

Al-Ghazzālī explains that the human soul has five faculties (sing: *quwwah*) or spirits. These are the sensory, the imaginative, the intelligential, the discursive, and the transcendental prophetic spirits.[170]They are all lights, because it is through them that objects of various kinds and realities of various levels are perceived. They pertain to man's cognitive powers. Employing the symbolism inherent in the Light Verse,

---

169. See al-Ghazzālī, *Mishkāt al-anwār*, p. 157. Some scholars maintain that the figure of veils in the hadith is not 70,000 but 700.

170. Al-Ghazzālī, *Mishkāt al-anwār*, pp. 143-149.

al-Ghazzālī identifies its five symbols - niche (*mishkāt*), glass (*zujājah*), lamp (*miṣbāḥ*), tree (*shajarah*), and oil (*zaytu*) - with the five faculties of the human soul. He maintains that the niche symbolizes the sensory spirit, the glass the imaginative spirit, the lamp the intelligential spirit, the tree the ratiocinative or discursive spirit, and the oil the transcendental Prophetic spirit.[171]Al-Ghazzālī argues that it is by virtue of the microcosmic fact that the lights of the spirit are graded one rank above another that the Light Verse uses the phrase "light upon light" through which man is guided to the Divine Light.[172]

According to al-Ghazzālī, man can be veiled both by light and darkness or by a mixture of the two. Having explained the meaning of the grades of light in the human soul, he sought to do the same with the grades of darkness by interpreting the Darkness Verse. He draws our attention first of all to the symbolism of the fathomless ocean (*baḥr lujjiy*). It symbolizes "the world of mortal dangers, of evil chances, of blinding trouble."[173] The phenomena of the darkness of the ocean described in the Verse are for the science of oceanography to explore and discover their secrets. From the symbolical point of view, however, the "first billow (*mawj*)" is the "wave of lust, whereby souls acquire the bestial attributes, and are occupied with sensual pleasures, and the satisfaction of worldly ambitions."[174] This wave of lust represents darkness, since it

171. Al-Ghazzālī, *Mishkāt al-anwār*, pp. 150-154.

172. Al-Ghazzālī, *Mishkāt al-anwār*, p. 154.

173. Al-Ghazzālī, *Mishkāt al-anwār*, p. 155.

174. Al-Ghazzālī cited the following verse as the scriptural basis of his interpretation: "...they enjoy [this world] and eat as cattle eat; and Hell will

makes the soul both blind and deaf.

The "second billow" is the "wave of ferocious attributes, which impel the soul to wrath, enmity, hatred, prejudice, envy, boastfulness, ostentation, pride." This wave too is a symbol of darkness. It is above the first billow, because "anger is stronger than lust," which "cannot for a moment stand up against anger at its height."[175] On top of the second billow is "the clouds" (*saḥāb*), which symbolize "rank beliefs, lying heresies, corrupt imaginings, which become so many veils veiling the unbeliever from the true faith, from knowledge of the Real, and from illumination by the sunlight of the Qur'an and human intelligence."[176]It is the property of a cloud to veil the shining of the sunlight. It is because all the three levels of waves are zones of darkness that the Qur'an uses the phrase "darkness one above another."

---

be their abode," chapter 47 ("Muḥammad"), verse 12. See *Mishkāt al-anwār*, p. 155.

175. Al-Ghazzālī, *Mishkāt al-anwār*, pp. 155-156.

176. Al-Ghazzālī, *Mishkāt al-anwār*, p. 156.

*Chapter Seven*

# The Human Microcosm in the Qur'an: The Universe within Man

## Introduction

It is our intention in this chapter to provide a comprehensive explanation of the idea of microcosm and discuss its Qur'anic foundation in a detailed manner. The idea of microcosm has an important epistemological role in traditional Islamic science. It finds numerous applications in a wide range of fields of knowledge and sectors of human civilization, particularly medicine, architecture, alchemy, psychology, science of society, and political thought. Hopefully, through a wider and a better appreciation of this idea and its underlying epistemology as well as its applications, which has proved to be timeless in its relevance and usefulness to human thought, we would be able to resurrect it in our contemporary world with a new and more abiding lease of life in the world of ideas that will serve as an indispensable intellectual tool in the twenty-first century agenda of renewal of human civilization (*tajdīd al-haḍārī*).

## The Meaning of Microcosm

The English word 'microcosm' is etymologically derived from a combination of two Greek words, *mikros* which means little and *kosmos* which means universe. Thus microcosm means in English "the little world" or "the miniature universe."[177] The word is used with this meaning both in relation to man as an individual and man as society or community. Man is regarded as the "epitome of the universe" in the same way society or community may be regarded as one. The description of both man and society as 'microcosm' was particularly emphasized in the pre-modern period in the West[178] and even more so in traditional Islamic civilization. The word microcosm was used as a scientific term in many traditional Islamic sciences and arts, particularly in natural and political sciences[179]. In the latter part of the modern period, the word acquired another meaning when it is used in ecology to mean "a small ecosystem." In this book, however, our concern is with the idea of the microcosm understood in reference to the individual man or "man as such" rather than in reference to man viewed

177. See Michael Agnes, editor in chief, *Webster's New World College Dictionary* (New York: Macmillan USA, 1997), fourth edition, p. 909.

178. For references to the usage of the concept of microcosm in the medieval West see Henry Bett, *Johannes Scotus Erigena, A Study in Medieval Philosophy* (Cambridge: Cambridge University Press, 1925; reprinted 1964).

179. Among the classical Muslim scientists who used the idea of microcosm extensively as a scientific concept were members of the *Ikhwān al-Ṣafā'*. Their most well-known works titled *Rasā'il* ("The Epistles") contain a lot of discussions on this idea and concept with applications to a number of the sciences. In Islamic political science, al-Fārābī and Ibn Rushd were the outstanding thinkers who spoke of society as a microcosm.

in his collective or societal setting.

In Islamic thought, the Arabic word used to signify the microcosm is *al-'ālam al-ṣaghīr*, which literally also means "the small world or cosmos." The word does not occur in the Qur'an. In fact, as we have indicated in chapter three, the word *'ālam* in the singular is not found in the Qur'an. Instead, it is the word *al-'ālamīn*, its plural that occurs many times in the Qur'an in which it is usually understood to signify the cosmos. The coinage of the term *al-'ālam al-ṣaghīr* was attributed to 'Alī ibn Abī Ṭālib, a cousin, a son-in-law, and a companion of the Prophet (salutation and peace be upon him), and one of the earliest exegetical authorities in Islam. Although this term is not found in the Qur'an the idea of microcosm that it seeks to convey, as understood by 'Alī himself, is in full accord with the total Qur'anic view of man. We maintain that if all the verses in the Qur'an pertaining to the various aspects and dimensions of the human constitution are collected together and then reflected on synthetically with a keen and intuitive intellect, then one would reach the same inevitable conclusion as arrived at by 'Alī, namely that man is indeed a microcosm. In other words, the human constitution viewed as a whole is essentially identical to the whole of the objective universe external to man. In the light of this assertion we may then seek to revive in our century the traditional claim that man is indeed a complete and perfect replica of the universe, albeit in miniature form.

Interestingly, in the Qur'an there is a reference to how God compares between His creation of the Universe and of man for the purpose of human reflection and contemplation. The Qur'an poses this question to man: "What! Are you the more difficult to create (*a'antum ashaddu khalqan*) or the heaven [above] (*al-samā'*)? God has constructed (*banā*) it: on high has

He raised its canopy (*samk*) and He has given it order and perfection (*sawwāhā*)."[180] This verse tells us that, if the two Divine creations are to be conceived and compared in human terms,[181] then man the microcosm[182] is easier to create than the universe the macrocosm.[183] The reason for it seems obvious and logical. When it comes to human creations the norm is that it is always easier to create the replica of an inspired original piece of art work than to create the original itself, regardless of the intended size of the replica. But the just quoted verse amounts to a divine permission to man to make comparisons between

180. *The Qur'an*, chapter 79 ("Those Who Tear Out"), verses 27-28.

181. Although the source of the comparison is divine, the comparison itself is necessarily formulated in terms that can easily be understood by the human mind, since the very purpose of the comparison is to impress upon man a sense of awe and wonder of God, especially of His Knowledge, Power and Wisdom as manifested in the two creations. From the divine point of view, however, everything is easy. As the Qur'an emphasizes, it is sufficient for God to give His creative command "kun!" and there "it is." There are eight verses in the Qur'an that refer to the Divine command "kun!" One verse reads: "[God is] the Originator (*badī'u*) of the heavens and the earth. When He decrees a matter He only says to it "Be," and it is." See chapter 2, ("The Cow"), verse 117. For the other verses see Chapter One, note 16. However, as to be explained below in the main text, the quoted verse envisages comparative divine creative works that exclude creations from nothing.

182. Man the microcosm is inferred from the word *antum* in the verse, which in the second person plural is used here to address every member of the human or Adamic species.

183. The Universe the macrocosm is inferred from the word *al-samā'*, which in the singular can also mean the whole firmament as contrasted with the earth. See Chapter Three where this issue is discussed in details.

two or more divine works in terms of their complexity and difficulty to create as seen from both divine and human perspectives and thus in terms of the extent of knowledge involved.

A comparison between two divine works such as between the macrocosmic universe and man the microcosm may be made at several levels. The most problematic level would be the one in which the element of creation *ex nihilo* ("creation out of nothing") is brought into the discussion. At this level of comparison the macrocosmic universe would be viewed as a divine work of art with an original stuff that was created from nothing (*'adam*) whereas man the microcosm would be presented as being created from pre-existing things. As the Qur'an says: "[God] is the Originator (*badī'u*) of the heavens and the earth from nothing"[184] and "We created (*khalaqnā*) man from sounding clay, from mud molded into shape."[185] The idea of creation from nothing necessitates the acceptance of metaphysical or theological beliefs that for most people could not be rationally understood. Creating things from nothing is the divine prerogative alone. The limited creative power that God has given man in accordance with the principle "God created Ādam in His image" does not include the power to emulate Him in creating things from nothing. Since creations are always understood by the human mind to be from pre-existing things, if the main purpose of God making comparisons of His own works of creation is to provide educational instructions to man, then these comparisons must be in such wise that they are within the reach of human

---

184. *The Qur'an*, chapter 2 ("The Cow"), verse 117.

185. *The Qur'an*, chapter 15 ("The Rocky Tract"), verse 26.

comprehension and even scientific verification. For this reason, in the verse under discussion, the comparison between the divine creations of the macrocosm and the microcosm is brought down to a simpler level, which is the level of creation that is meant by the term *khalqan*. At this level of comparison we human beings may appeal to scientific contribution for epistemological help and enlightenment, especially through cosmogony, the science of the origin and birth of the universe in the case of the macrocosm and through physical anthropology in the case of the creation of Ādam (peace be upon him), the first man or the first human microcosm on earth and the creation of Eve his wife,[186] and embryology[187] in

186. The origin of the first man and the first woman, who according to revealed traditions got married and bore children, is a complex and indeed mysterious issue that is beyond the competence of science alone to satisfactorily solve it. Science needs an invaluable help from both revealed religion and traditional philosophy if it were to unravel more and more dimensions and elements of the mystery. However, the nature of the mystery is such that even if science and religion and philosophy were to work together in providing its answers it is almost certain that there would always be a part of it that remains unsolvable, thus implying that under such circumstances spiritual faith, which could be an enlightened one, seems to be the only rational choice left open to human beings. According to traditional Islamic cosmology, sex and its differentiation into the male and the female pair possess both a macrocosmic and a microcosmic dimension.

187. Notwithstanding the modern interpretation of the human embryological process as a clear proof of the theory of biological evolution, there is the traditional perspective in Islamic science that interprets the same process as the progressive unfolding of the hierarchical microcosmic order and reality beginning with the mineral order to ascend through the plant and animal living forms to the distinctively human life form simultaneous to the ensoulment of the embryo.

the case of their descendants who inherit their microcosmic nature.

The Qur'an is found to be using different words to denote different types, stages and processes of creation. Unlike in the English language where the same general term 'creation' is used to denote them all the Qur'anic Arabic is judicious in its choice of terms when describing the different stages and processes of creation. Thus, for example, with respect to God's creative activities, the word *bada'a* or the more widely used *abda'* and its derivatives would convey the meaning of "originating or creating from nothing." The word *khalaqa* which is often loosely translated by many people as "he created" actually refers to a particular stage of creation from pre-existing things with its attending processes, and not to the whole facets of creation. As discussed in Chapter One, the primary meaning of *khalaqa* is "measuring or determining the measure, proportion, or the like of a thing; and the making of a thing by measure, or according to the measure of another thing; or proportioning a thing to another thing."[188] In the light of this core meaning of *khalaqa* it becomes clear that comparing two divine works of creation both at the level of *khalqan* would allow a spacious room for scientific verification of the revealed data on the subject. Also referred to in the same Chapter is the Qur'an's invitation to man to verify for himself God's claim on the flawlessness in the heavens or macrocosm He has created.[189] However, this is the first and perhaps the only time that we are encountering in the Qur'an God's invitation to man to undertake a comparative study of two of His most important

188. See Chapter One, notes 18-23.

189. *The Qur'an*, chapter 67 ("The Dominion"), verse 3.

creations, namely the macrocosm and the microcosm.

In many spiritual traditions, man is viewed as a microcosm on the justification that he is a small universe in which, essentially speaking, all of its elements are gathered together in an ordered way that is analogous to the macrocosmic order itself. The Qur'anic idea of the microcosm is not established on the basis of explicit meanings provided by one or two particular verses. In fact, we will never find such verses that are limited to just one or two of them, precisely because they do not exist. There are, however, several specific verses that allude to the idea of microcosm, and we will cite and discuss a good number of them later in this chapter. These alluding verses, however, could not by themselves establish the Qur'anic basis of the idea of microcosm in a conclusive manner. We need to gather all the verses of the Qur'an that speak of the creation of every essential aspect of man, physical or otherwise. This is what we intend to do in this chapter, since it is these multiple and diverse aspects of man gathered as such that we are going to present as the constituent elements of the microcosm. Going through the whole Qur'an, we find that there is no verse dealing with the creation of man that does so by explicitly addressing or treating the whole constitution of man. Rather, each of these verses speaks of only some aspects or elements of the human constitution, even though it may be true that in some verses the aspects referred to are quite comprehensive in scope.

We propose to establish in this chapter the Qur'anic basis of the idea of microcosm by showing that there is a necessary and sufficient set or collection of verses that when viewed together will clearly be seen as addressing the issue of the "complete man." This total constitution of man will depict itself as comprising in an essential manner all the constituent creatures or elements of the universe. It is to be observed that all the relevant verses are found scattered in the Qur'an, beginning in the "Opening Chapter" (*Sūrat al-Fātiḥah*) right through all its pages to its very ending in the last chapter itself, the "Chapter on Mankind" (*Sūrat al-Nās*).[190] It goes without saying that the search for the relevant verses presupposes sufficient knowledge of the essential components of the universe. This knowledge has been presented in the preceding chapters of this work. The universe comprises essentially three qualitatively different worlds, namely the physical world, the spiritual and angelic worlds, and the subtle world that is intermediate between them. Corresponding to this essential composition of the universe is the total reality of the human being that embraces elements of [1] the material or physical world, [2] the biological world, including plant and animal souls, [3] the subtle world of the jinn, [4] the world of the angels or the intellects (*'uqūl*), and [5] a spiritual substance from the Divine Breath referred to in the Qur'an as *min rūḥī*.[191]

Man as the microcosm is traditionally understood as the counterpart of the universe that is external to the individual man, which is called the macrocosm, meaning "the big cosmos" (*al-'ālam al-kabīr*). This multi-level and multi-dimensional

---

190. The last chapter is the 114th, consisting of only six short verses and thus making it one of the shortest chapters of the Qur'an.

191. The idea of the Divine Breath as the source of the human spirit (*rūḥ*) is made clear by this verse of the Qur'an: "When I have fashioned him [*i.e.* Ādam] [in due proportion] (*sawwaytuhu*) and breathed into him of My spirit, fall ye down in obeisance unto him" (chapter 15, verse 29); see also chapter 38, verse 72.

relationship between man and the universe external to him constitutes one of the most fundamental cosmological principles of Islam that its intellectual culture has shown in its history to have profound implications for both the sciences of man and the sciences of the universe. The essential one-to-one correspondence between the macrocosm and the microcosm also has implications for epistemology. The main implication is that a true knowledge of the various levels of macrocosmic reality would demand the exercise of the corresponding levels of man's cognitive powers inherent within his hierarchic microcosmic reality and consciousness. Hence, no knowledge of deeper levels of cosmic reality could be possible without man as the knower or subject of knowledge fathoming into his own inner cognitive consciousness and igniting his latent inner cognitive faculties or powers. If man does not seek to actualize his latent cognitive powers that lie beyond the powers of his physical senses and lower imagination and his rational power of ratiocination, then he has to be content with merely acquiring the lower kind of empirical knowledge of the universe, which to our mind is the unfortunate lot of modern science.

However, the Qur'an makes it very clear that God did not create the universe just to enable man to acquire such a kind of knowledge alone. It also points to the possibility of another kind of knowledge of the universe – a metaphysical one – which in reality is also empirical in nature if by "empirical knowledge" we mean one that is based on experience.[192] The

---

192. In the West itself, we meet thinkers who speak of these two types of empirical knowledge. The medieval English philosopher-scientist, Roger Bacon (c. 1214-1294), who was considerably influenced by the philosophy of Ibn Sīnā whom he called "the leader and prince of philosophy after

main difference to be noted between the two forms of "empirical" knowledge of the universe pertains to the distinction between the natures and grades of the two knowledge experiences. Metaphysical knowledge of the universe may be regarded as of a higher kind of empirical knowledge, since it results from the use of higher human faculties of knowing, namely the faculties of spiritual cognition and intellectual intuition. It is viewed as superior to the kind of empirical knowledge that is ordinarily understood, especially when it is judged in the light of man's obligatory spiritual and intellectual needs and in the light of his final return to his Creator. The traditional idea of the microcosm and its one-to-one correspondence with the macrocosm served as a constant reminder to Muslim men of science of the multi-dimensional and multi-level nature of human knowledge of the universe. It was also in the light of the microcosm that a number of classical Muslim thinkers such as Ikhwān al-Ṣafā', al-Ghazzālī and Ibn al-'Arabī have accepted the idea of the universe as "the big man" (*al-insān al-kabīr*).[193] This idea has proved to be a

---

Aristotle," spoke of two types of experimentation. The first type of experiment is the one that man makes on nature external to him. The other kind is the experiment that he performs on his own inner nature. See Osman Bakar, *Tawhid and Science*, p. 150.

193. Ikhwān al-Ṣafā' said, "... The sages (*al-ḥukamā'*) also call it [*i.e.* the universe (*al-'ālam*)] the great man (*al-insān al-kabīr*). See Ikhwān al-Ṣafā', *Risalah* (Cairo: 'Arabiyah Press, 1928), vol. II, p. 20, cited by Seyyed Hossein Nasr, *An Introduction to Islamic Cosmological Doctrines*, p. 67. Ibn al-'Arabī referred to the idea of the universe as "the great man" in the following words: "the cosmos is one of the people, since it is the human being great in size ..." See William C. Chittick, *The Self-Disclosure of God*, p. 289. He further says, "The angels in respect to the whole cosmos are like the forms

very useful conceptual tool in the understanding of cosmic reality.

### The Idea of Microcosm in the Qur'an

There are a number of passages in the Qur'an alluding to the idea of microcosm. By a Qur'anic passage we mean a set of successive verses that collectively deals with a common theme, which in this particular case is the theme of microcosm. We may thus speak here of a thematic passage the proper understanding of which would require a "thematic exegesis" (*al-tafsīr al-mawḍūʿī*). Altogether we are able to identify nine such thematic passages in the whole Qur'an, not all of which are explicit. However, we may infer from the even not so explicit verses in some of the identified passages that they actually refer to the reality of the microcosm. For the purpose of clarity in our references to these nine passages we are now designating them with letters arranged in an alphabetical order corresponding to an ascending numerical order of their respective chapters of occurrence in the Qur'an (see Table below):

---

manifest within man's imagination, as also are the jinn. *So the cosmos is a great human being* (italics mine) only through the *wujūd* of the perfect human being, who is its rationally speaking soul ..." (p. 289).

**Table of Microcosm Passages in the Qur'an**

| Passage | Chapter Number | Chapter Name | Verses |
|---|---|---|---|
| A | 1 | The Opening Chapter (Sūrat al-Fātiḥah) | 5 – 7 |
| B | 2 | The Cow (Sūrat al-Baqarah) | 30 – 39 |
| C | 7 | The Heights (Sūrat al-A'rāf) | 10 – 25 |
| D | 15 | The Rocky Tract (Sūrat al-Ḥijr) | 26 – 43 |
| E | 20 | Ṭā Ḥā (Sūrat Ṭā Ḥā) | 115 – 127 |
| F | 32 | The Prostration (Sūrat al-Sajdah) | 7 – 9 |
| G | 38 | Ṣād (Sūrat Ṣād) | 71 – 85 |
| H | 95 | The Fig (Sūrat al-Tīn) | 4 – 6 |
| J | 96 | The Clinging Clot or Read (Sūrat al-'Alaq or Iqrā') | 1 – 19 (the whole chapter) |

These passages are of varying lengths, some long and others relatively short. However, even the very short ones, despite their brevity, do not fail to impress us with their remarkably concise descriptions of the length and breadth of the microcosmic constitution of man as such (*insān*) and yet rich in meanings. In our considered view, as we shall show in the following pages, these are the passages that, when taken together, provide a clear picture of the structure and major components of the whole human microcosm. For easy cross-references, we also decide to reproduce these passages prior to discussing them. We will discuss in this chapter all the above nine passages, albeit insofar as they throw light on our understanding of the idea of microcosm in its various dimensions.

**The Idea of Microcosm in the Opening Chapter (Passage A)**

The first such alluding passage in the Qur'an, denoted as Passage A in the above table, is in the Opening Chapter (*Sūrat al-Fātiḥah*) itself. The passage reads:

> You alone we worship, and your help alone we seek (1:5)
>
> Guide us upon the straight path (1:6)
>
> The path of those on whom You have bestowed Your grace, those whose [portion] is not anger, and who do not go astray (1:7)

Man as a species is not explicitly mentioned in the chapter, but its existence is implied by the second pronoun in the plural, namely the word "we" (*naḥnu*) in verse 1:5 and the word "us" (*na*) in verse 1:6. Verse 1:5 says: "You alone we worship (*na'budu*), and your help alone we seek (*nasta'īn*)." And verse 1:6 says: "Guide us (*ihdinā*) upon the straight path." Furthermore, verse 1:7 states a threefold spiritual classification of mankind[194] that is perennial in the sense that it is true at all times. So the passage comprising the three verses 1:5-7 may be interpreted as referring to the whole of mankind. Significantly, we thus have in the form of this chapter an essential summary of the Qur'an in which man is the only species of creatures mentioned, apart from the word *'ālamīn* that signifies the whole universe.

We may then argue that the chapter alludes to man as the microcosm for two main reasons. First, since by inference man is the only species mentioned in the Opening Chapter and this chapter summarizes the whole Qur'an, we may advance the interpretation that man represents the whole creation. Second, according to an interpretation popular among the Sufis, the words "we" and "us" in verses 1:5 and 1:6 may be understood to mean the whole creation. According to this interpretation, every time man performs the canonical prayer (*ṣalāt*), he recites the Opening Chapter in full, which is a must according

194. Through the verses 1:6-7 the Opening Chapter introduces us to the first of several spiritual classifications of mankind that are found in the Qur'an. The classification given in this Chapter concerns the overall unchanging pattern of man's exercise of his moral freedom in leading his earthly life. With respect to the exercise of this moral choice the Qur'an discerns three groups of people throughout human history. First, the group of people who are said to be on "the straight path" (*ṣirāt al-mustaqīm*) by virtue of which they are characterized as recipients of Divine Grace (*ni'mah*). The Qur'an defines the straight path as the path of life that is devoted to the worship and service (*'ibādah*) of the One God. For this definition see, for example, *The Qur'an*, chapter 36 ("Yā Sīn"), verse 61. Second, the very opposite of the first group whose characteristic lot is incurring the divine anger on account of their opposition to and rebellion of the straight path and all that it symbolizes and represents. And third, the group of people who have erred from the straight path.

to the canons of Islamic *ṣalāt* without which it would be deemed invalid by the Divine Law (*al-Sharīʿah*), and in reciting the verses 1:5 and 1:6 in the name "we" he is addressing God in the name of all creation. The rationale of this interpretation is that even when the individual man is offering the prayer alone he still utters the word "we" and not "I" as dictated by the Opening Chapter. The implication of the verses 1:5 and 1:6 is that man is given the honor of praying to God in the name of all creation by virtue of the fact that, as a creature, he is the "epitome of the cosmos."

The above arguments that are presented as an affirmation of the idea of man as a microcosm are essential in nature, taken as it were from the essence of the Qur'an itself. These essential arguments are, however, explained in a more detailed manner in other parts of the Qur'an. What we mean by this statement is that the idea of man as microcosm is alluded to in a clearer way in certain passages of the Qur'an and presented in an even more explicit manner in the collection of verses dealing with the creation of man in his various dimensions.

## The Idea of Microcosm in the Chapter of the Cow (Passage B)

The Passage B comprising the verses 30-39 of the second chapter, *Sūrat al-Baqarah* ("Chapter of the Cow") is the second significant passage in the Qur'an to allude to the idea of human microcosm in a general way but, unlike the allusion in *Sūrah al-Fātiḥah*, it provides more specific pointers to the idea. This passage is about the creation of Ādam (peace be upon him!) as God's vicegerent (*khalīfah*) on the planet Earth and, by "natural" extension, the likewise creation of all his descendants,[195] who are referred to in traditional sources as the Adamic (*ādamī*) species.[196]

Comprising ten verses, Passage B may be best comprehended if it were to be read and interpreted together with the remaining seven almost similar passages concerning either the creation of Ādam (peace be upon him!) as the first human being or of man (*insān*) in general that he symbolized or the reproduction of his progeny that will be cited and discussed later. While varying in lengths all these passages provide a concise description of the length and breadth of the microcosmic constitution of man as such (*insān*).

Passage B reads as follows:

Behold, your Lord said to the angels: "I will create a

---

195. That both the honor and responsibility of being God's *khalīfah* on earth is given not just to Ādam (peace be upon him!) but rather to the whole human species that sprang from him is made clearer by three other verses in the Qur'an, where the word *khalīfah* occurs in the plural (*khalā'if*). One of these verses, chapter 6 ("The Cattle"), verse 165, says: "For, He it is who has made you [His] agents and inheritors of the Earth (*khalā'if al-arḍ*) and has raised you in ranks, some above others ..." See also verse 62, chapter 27 ("The Ant") where the phrase *khulafā' al-arḍ* is used and verse 39, chapter 35 ("The Originator") where again the phrase *khalā'if* occurs. Admittedly, given the several senses conveyed by the word *khalīfah*, the context of each of the four verses in view (including verse 2:30) may suggest one sense as being more appropriate than another for its case.

196. The Qur'an uses the term *banī Ādam* (literally, children of Ādam) to signify the "Adamic race or species." Out of the twenty-five occurrences of the name Ādam in the Qur'an, eight of them are in the form of the phrase *banī Ādam* . The Adamic species is identical to what is called "mankind" or "human species" which are signified by the Qur'anic terms *al-insān*, *al-ins*, and *al-nās*.

vicegerent (*khalīfah*) on earth." They said: "Will Thou place therein one who will make mischief therein and shed blood while we celebrate Thy praises and glorify thy holy [name]? He said: "I know what you know not" (2:30).

And He taught Ādam the names (*al-asmā'*) of all things; then He placed them before the angels, and said: "Tell me the names of these if you are right" (2:31).

They said: "Glory to Thee, of knowledge we have none, save what Thou has taught us: In truth it is Thou Who are perfect in knowledge and wisdom" (2:32).

He said: "O Ādam! tell them their names." When he had told them, God said: Did I not tell you that I know the secrets of heaven and earth, and I know what you reveal and what you conceal?" (2:33).

And behold, We said to the angels: "Bow down to Ādam" and they bowed down. Not so Iblīs: he refused and was haughty: he was of those who reject faith (2:34).

We said: "O Ādam! Dwell you and your wife in the Garden; and eat of the bountiful things therein as [where and when] you will; but do not approach this tree, or you run into harm and transgression" (2:35).

Then did Satan make them slip (*azallahuma*) from the [Garden], and get them out of the state [of felicity] in which they had been. We said: "Get you down, all [you people], with enmity between yourselves. On earth will be your dwelling-place and your means of livelihood – for a time" (2:36).

Then learnt (*talaqqā*) Ādam from his Lord words of inspiration (*kalimāt*), and his Lord turned toward him;

for He is Oft-Returning (*al-Tawwāb*), Most Merciful (*al-Raḥīm*) (2:37)

We said: "Get you down all from here; and if, as is sure, there comes to you Guidance (*hudan*) from Me, whosoever follows My guidance, on them shall be no fear, nor shall they grieve" (2:38).

"But those who reject faith and belie Our Signs, they shall be companions of the Fire; they shall abide therein" (2:39).

The above passage B points to the whole constitution of the first human being, Ādam (peace be upon him!) as a microcosm. The most fundamental pointer to this microcosmic constitution is the creation of Ādam (peace be upon him!) as God's *khalīfah* on earth. The idea of *khalīfah* – whether it is to be understood as vicegerent, agent, inheritor, or successor,[197] but more particularly when understood as vicegerent – implies the interrelated meanings of superiority, supremacy, dominance, and mastery. Ādam's superiority and supremacy over all other creatures is made clear in the above passage by the verse 2:34 which tells us of the Divine Command to the angels and the subtle creatures, of which Iblīs is one, to bow down to him. All the angels bowed down to Ādam (peace be upon him!) and so did all the creatures of the subtle world with the exception of Iblīs (Satan). Since the angels have been created by God to faithfully administer the worlds below them in accordance with His Plan and Will, Ādam's superiority and

---

197. For a detailed discussion of the meanings of *khalīfah* on the basis of its classical Arabic usage, see Edward W. Lane, *Arabic-English Lexicon*, vol. 1, pp. 797-798.

supremacy over them would mean that it is over the whole of creation. The refusal of Iblīs to bow down to Ādam (peace be upon him!) in defiance of God's Command presented, however, the greatest challenge to him and his descendants in the execution and fulfillment of their function and role as *khalīfah* on earth.

Ādam's position as God's *khalīfah* on earth alludes to his special and unique constitution as a creature. He has to be cosmologically connected in some way with both the terrestrial and celestial worlds and also metaphysically connected to God Himself. Both the bowing down to Ādam (peace be upon him!) by the angels and the refusal by Satan to do so furnish us in this passage B with key information about the core components of the Adamic constitution. The angels bowed down to Ādam (peace be upon him!) only after they have been shown Ādam's superiority to them in terms of his knowledge capacity and the kind of knowledge that God has imparted to him (2:21-23). Their acknowledgment of Ādam's superiority in knowledge means that he was a sentient being endowed with cognitive powers and instruments that empowered him to receive and acquire the highest forms of knowledge that were beyond their reach. On the basis of evidence provided by the angels themselves (2:32), they acknowledged the fact that, by virtue of his capacity to know "the names of all things," Ādam (peace be upon him!) knew what they knew and also what they did not know. In other words, the Adamic constitution contains within itself cognitive instruments and powers that have both angelic and supra-angelic qualities. The angels' act of prostration before Ādam (peace be upon him!) symbolizes their acknowledgment of his superiority to them in the hierarchy of God's creatures.

Prior to their being shown Ādam's superiority in knowledge, the angels only saw his animal nature and constitution with negative tendencies to do mischief and shed blood that disqualify him from being positioned as God's *khalīfah* on earth, since these qualities stand opposed to their own spiritual qualities that befit this divine positioning. Through the angels' first response to God's positioning of Ādam (peace be upon him!) as His *khalīfah* on earth, we are informed that elements of the animal world form part of his constitution. Iblīs' refusal to bow down to Ādam (peace be upon him!) and its seduction of him and his wife, Eve, leading to the loss of their state of innocence and felicity (2:36), provide another source of information about the components of Ādam's constitution. Passage B does not tell us why Iblīs refused to bow down to Ādam (peace be upon him!), but the reason is given in passage C which we shall later reproduce in full and discuss. In this later passage Iblīs told God that he refused to bow down to Ādam (peace be upon him!) because, being created from fire, he has a better constitution than him, who was created from clay.

In contrast, in passage B the mention of Iblīs' disobedience of God's command to prostrate before Ādam (peace be upon him!) (2:34) is not accompanied with any information that would allow us to infer that clay is a core element of Ādam's constitution. Instead, the mention of Iblīs' disobedience in question is accompanied with a piece of information that points to the spiritual elements and dimension of Ādam's constitution. The accompanying information – "he [*i.e.* Iblīs] was of those who deny or reject faith (*kāna min al-kāfirīn*)" – is alluding to that part of Adamic constitution, which Iblīs seeks deliberately to reject and deny (2:34). This part could only mean the spiritual dimension of Ādam (peace be upon him!), since an acknowledgment of its reality by Iblīs would demolish his claim of superiority to Ādam. To prop up its false claim of superiority to Ādam (peace be upon him), Iblīs resorted to denying his spiritual dimension and reducing him to his lowest dimension, namely his physical dimension as symbolized by clay.

Where passage B makes a clearer but still a general kind of allusion to the terrestrial dimension of Ādam's constitution is in verses 2:30 and 2:36 which present Ādam (peace be upon him!) as an earthly creature and the same verse 2:36 that tells us of Satan's seduction of Ādam (peace be upon him!) and Eve that led to their "fall" from the paradisal state on earth to the state of enmity among their descendants. In verse 2:36, the allusion is to Ādam's lower soul (*nafs*), an essential component of his terrestrial constitution, the visible counterpart of which is his physical body generated from clay, since it was only through this lower soul that Satan's seductive power could be exercised on him and his wife and, by natural extension, on all human beings.

Ādam's spiritual dimension is further alluded to in passage B by the verses 2:37-38. These verses depict Ādam (peace be upon him!) as a spiritual being who was capable of understanding spiritual guidance from God and putting it in practical shape in his life on earth, thus justifying his position as His *khalīfah* on this unique planet. He was thus alluded to as being in possession of spiritual faculties that enabled him to develop the best of relationships with God such as to turn toward Him in repentance (*tawbah*) and ask for His forgiveness and to obey and love Him.

Passage B as a whole thus provides clear pointers and

allusions to the total constitution of Ādam (peace be upon him!) as microcosmic in nature. His constituent elements that are explicitly stated in the passage belong to the physical and animal worlds as well as the subtle world with which Iblīs or Satan is identified. In Islamic cosmology, on the basis of the Qur'an, the subtle world is understood as the world inhabited by the jinn species. The Qur'an makes clear that Iblīs belongs to the jinn species.[198] As for Ādam's constituent elements that are implicitly stated in the passage, these belong to the intellectual and spiritual worlds. These elements are either angelic or supra-angelic in nature and quality. Ādam's supra-angelic elements refer to his intellectual and spiritual knowledge and qualities that are beyond the angels' understanding. Essentially speaking, Ādam's constitution therefore comprises the whole cosmos, making him the first human microcosm.

## The Idea of Microcosm in the Chapter of the Heights (Passage C)

The third passage to be discussed – Passage C in our Table of Microcosm Passages – comprising sixteen verses in all, is contained in the chapter of the heights (*al-A'rāf*), which while repeating some of the ideas contained in Passage B provides more detailed pointers to Ādam's total constitution as a human microcosm.[199]

---

198. *The Qur'an*, chapter 18 ("The Cave"), verse 50.

199. From a more general consideration than our present interest in the relevance of the two passages to the discussion of man as the microcosm, Yusuf 'Ali made the following observation regarding the similarities and the differences between the two passages as well as between them and passages D and E: "In places the words are precisely the same, and yet the whole

The passage reads:

> It is We who have placed you with authority on earth (*makkannākum fi'l-arḍ*), and provided you therein with means for the fulfillment of your life (*ma'āyish*); small are the thanks that you give! (7:10).
>
> It is We who created you and gave your shape (*ṣawwarnākum*); then We bade the angels bow down to Ādam, and they bowed down; not so Iblīs; he refused to be of those who bow down (7:11).
>
> [God] said: "What prevented you from bowing down when I commanded you?" He said: "I am better than he: Thou created me from fire (*nār*), and him from clay (*ṭīn*)" (7:12).
>
> [God] said: "Get you down from this: it is not for you to be arrogant here: get out, for you are of the meanest [of creatures] (*al-ṣaghīrin*) (7:13).
>
> He said: "Give me respite till the day they are raised up" (7:14).
>
> [God] said: "Be you among those who have respite" (7:15).
>
> He said: "Because You have thrown me out of the Way, lo! I will lie in wait for them on your Straight Way" (7:16).

argument is different. In each case it exactly fits the context. In chapter 2 [*i.e.* passage B] the argument was about the origin of man. Here the argument is a prelude to his history on earth ..." See Yusuf 'Ali, *The Meaning of the Holy Qur'an*, note 1007, p. 285. However, both passages provide arguments that are supportive of the idea of man as the microcosm.

"Then will I assault them from before them and behind them, from their right and their left: nor will You find, in most of them, gratitude [for Your mercies]" (7:17).

[God] said: "Get out from this, disgraced and expelled. If any of them follow you – Hell will I fill with you all" (7:18).

"O Ādam! Dwell you and your wife in the Garden, and enjoy [its good things] as you wish: but do not approach this tree, or you run into harm and transgression" (7:19).

Then began Satan to whisper suggestions to them, bringing openly before their minds all their shame that was hidden from them [before]: he said: "Your Lord only forbade you this tree, lest you should become angels or such beings as live forever" (7:20).

And he swore to them both that he was their sincere adviser (7:21).

So by deceit (*bi-ghurūr*) he brought about their fall: when they tasted of the tree, their shame became manifest to them, and they began to sew together the leaves of the Garden over their bodies. And their Lord called unto them: "Did I not forbid you that tree, and tell you that Satan was an avowed enemy unto you?" (7:22).

They said: "Our Lord! We have wronged our own souls: If Thou forgive us not and bestow not upon us Thy Mercy, we shall certainly be lost" (7:23).

[God] said: "Get ye down with enmity between yourselves. On earth will be your dwelling-place and your means of livelihood – for a time" (7:24)

> He said: "Therein shall you live, and therein shall you die; but from it shall you be taken out [at last]" (7:25).

In repeating the themes brought up in Passage B either in a slightly different or more substantive way, the Passage C just cited helps to strengthen the arguments for the soundness of the idea of human microcosm. These repeated themes are namely the themes of man as an earthly creature, the angels' prostration before Ādam (peace be upon him!), Iblīs' refusal to bow down to him, the spiritual fall of Ādam and Eve at the hands of Satan, the road to the recovery of their lost status of innocence and bliss referred to earlier as the paradisal state, and the earth as man's temporary home. It is quite clear that Passage C provides further explanations and clarifications of each of these subthemes. At the same time, this passage throws further light on Ādam's microcosmic constitution.

As in passage B, passage C through the verses 7:10 and 7:24-25) emphasizes the established position of Ādam (peace be upon him!) and his descendants as an earthly species having a whole range of physical and biological needs. Living as he was on earth, Ādam (peace be upon him!) had to possess a physical body, just like all other living creatures on this planet. While Passage B alludes to Ādam's physical body in a very general way,[200] Passage C makes quite explicit references[201] to it. There

---

200. The allusion to Ādam's physical body is said to be made in a general way in the sense that its existence is only implied by the following revealed data in the passage in question: [1] Ādam (peace be upon him!) has to live on earth (2:30); [2] he is partly an animal that sheds blood (*yasfiku al-dimā'*) on earth (2:30); [3] he consumes food and enjoys the physical comforts of living (*wa kulā minhā raghadā*) (2:35); [4] he is in need of a home or dwelling-place (*mustaqarr*) and various kinds of goods to serve his earthly life (*matāʿ*) (2:36).

201. However, Passage C repeats three of the above general allusions in passage B, namely allusions [1] (7:10), [3] (7:19), and [4] (7:24), and adds [5] one new general allusion to Ādam as a creature with a physical body when it refers to the Earth as the place where the human species live and die (7:25). But, as we shall now show, it also makes explicit references to Ādam's possession of a physical body. It may be observed that there are fine variations in the repetition of general allusions and pointers [1], [3], and [4]. In pointer [1] (2:30) Ādam's established position as an earthly creature is made clear in the statement "I am about to create a *khalīfah* on earth" (*innī jā'ilun fi'l-arḍ khalīfah*). In verse 7:10, pointer [1] is expressed in this way: "We have placed you with authority on earth" (*makkannā kum fi'l-arḍ*). This verse may be understood as a clarification (*tibyān*) and exposition (*tafsīl*) of verse 2:30, since the whole meanings of the verb *makkanā* explain the various dimensions of man's *khilāfah* (vicegerency) on earth, and it clarifies the position of the first man on earth, Ādam (peace be upon him!) as *khalīfah* as of such a nature as to be inherited by all his descendants, meaning the whole human species.

Pointer [3] in verses 2:35 and 7:19 is expressed in exactly the same words except that the word *raghadā* is not mentioned in the latter verse. Pointer [4] in verses 2:36, 7:10 and 7:24, however, shows both similarity and variation in expression. The sentence "On earth will be your dwelling-place and your means of livelihood – for a time" (*wa lakum fi'l-arḍ mustaqarr wa matā' ilā ḥīn*) occurs in both verses 2:36 and 7:24. But the part of 7:10 that serves as pointer [4] reads as follows: "And We provided you therein [*i.e.* on earth] with ways and means for the fulfillment of your life" (*Wa ja'alnā lakum fihā ma'āyish*). Meaning-wise, there are fine distinctions between the words *matā'* and *ma'āyish*. Yusuf 'Ali translates *matā'* as "means of livelihood" and *ma'āyish* as "means for the fulfillment of life." He understands *ma'āyish* as referring to "all the material things which are necessary to sustain, beautify, and refine life, as well as all those powers, faculties, and opportunities which are instrumental in bringing up life to a higher plane and preparing man for his high spiritual destiny." See Yusuf 'Ali, *The Meaning of the Holy Qur'an*, p. 25, verse 2:36, note 54 and p. 282, verse 7:10, note 995. In our view, Yusuf 'Ali has managed to capture the

are three such references. The first explicit reference in question is to the creation of Ādam's physical body from clay (*ṭīn*) (7:12). The second such reference is to the human shape and form (*ṣūrah*) given to Ādam's body (7:11). And the third such reference is to Ādam (peace be upon him!) and his wife "sewing together the leaves of the Garden (*waraq al-jannah*) over their bodies" to cover their shame (7:22). From the point of view of our discussion of Ādam's microcosmic constitution, the key word here is "clay." However, this word is not explained in Passage C. For information about the nature and constituents of clay we have to rely on some other passages to which we shall refer later. As we shall see later, the significance of the Qur'an's identification of Ādam's physical body with clay lies in the fact that clay in its various forms constitutes the microcosm of the physical world.

On the theme of the angels' prostration before Ādam (peace be upon him!), Passages B and C give the same reason for their prostration, namely Ādam's superiority, but this reason is highlighted in the two cases from different angles. In Passage B the angels bowed down to Ādam (peace be upon him!) in acknowledgment of his superiority in knowledge, whereas in Passage C (verse 7:12) the reason cited for it is his unique and superior form. The two cited reasons are not contradictory but rather they explain each other, only of course

---

whole meaning conveyed by the word *ma'āyish*, thereby showing its distinction from the word *matā'*. We hasten to add that, on the basis of the linguistic structures of the two verses in question, *matā'* and *ma'āyish* may be understood as referring to two forms or states of material culture, the former to a lower one for the purpose of bodily gratification and transient enjoyment, and the latter to a higher one for the purpose of spiritual, intellectual, and aesthetic satisfactions.

if we understand the shape and form that God gave Ādam (peace be upon him!) as not limited to his physical body. The idea of Ādam (peace be upon him!) as also having non-physical forms – more precisely spiritual-intellectual forms – is supported by both tradition and reason. Ādam's superiority in knowledge means that he possesses superior and more perfect knowledge capacity and cognitive instruments and powers, which presuppose his possession of superior intellectual-rational and spiritual forms that could serve as the receiver and container of knowledge of the "names of all things" taught by God and knowledge acquired through his own discovery. Equivalently, Ādam's superiority in form – an interpretation of verse 7:12 that is supported by verse 95:4 in Passage H and the Prophetic hadith on the creation of Ādam (peace be upon him!) in God's image or form – would mean among other things a superiority over all other creatures in the quality of both his knowledge container or capacity and content.

As especially emphasized in the Sufi spiritual and intellectual tradition, the Adamic form is the most perfect of all the creaturely forms, since it reflects God's Names and Qualities in the most integral manner. Thus, the Adamic form is both physical and spiritual-intellectual in nature. It is this spiritual-intellectual dimension of the Adamic form resulting from the blowing of the divine Spirit into Ādam's body and with its imprints of the Divine Names and Qualities that enabled him and human beings generally to acquire spiritual and intellectual virtues.

The themes of Iblīs' refusal to bow down to Ādam (peace be upon him!) and the fall of the latter and his wife at the hands of Satan furnish strong pointers to the existence of the last major dimension of the Adamic form, namely the subtle and psychic form. Just as Ādam's acquisition of spiritual and intellectual virtues presupposes the prior existence of spiritual forms in him that are to serve as their receptacle so does his newfound realm of consciousness, in which good and evil are freely mixed as a result of the "fall," presuppose the prior existence in the Adamic form of a subtle and psychic component that is to serve as the basis of its expansion into so many possible worlds. This particular realm of human consciousness is of great interest to both science and religion. Modern psychiatry, which is generally anti-religion and purely dependent on empirical approaches in the reductionistic sense to mental phenomena and the realm of consciousness, sees chaos in the psychic space of the human microcosm,[202] and infers from it that the whole of microcosmic reality is lawless and disorderly. And it does not know how to help someone trapped in the chaotic psychic space to get out of it and escape to the orderly higher world of peace, bliss and innocence. Islam as a religion provides man with the necessary knowledge and guidance to help him avoid or escape from the pitfalls of the subtle and psychic space that Passages A and B in the Qur'an attribute to Iblīs or Satan. In several of its other passages the Qur'an identifies the subtle and psychic space of the human microcosm in its various states and both in its positive and negative dimensions with the combined psychological space generated by the "self-reproaching soul"

202. Interestingly, as revealed by modern physics, there is an intermediate zone in the macrocosmic reality that is chaotic in nature between the qualitatively differentiated world and undifferentiated matter which is at its basis. This chaotic intermediate zone seems to correspond to the chaotic psychic and subtle space that is intermediate between the spiritual space of peace and order "above" it and the physical space observable to the senses that lies below it.

(*al-nafs al-lawwāmah*)[203] bordering upward with the spiritual space of the "tranquil soul" (*al-nafs al-muṭma'innah*)[204] and that generated by the "prone to evil soul" (*al-nafs la-ammārah*)[205] bordering below it.

The various traditional schools of Islamic psychology generally succeeded in harmonizing the perspectives of science and those of the Qur'an on the subject of the human soul and consciousness. The kind of scientific psychology founded and developed by such classical Muslim philosophers and scientists as al-Fārābī, Ibn Sīnā, Ikhwān al-Ṣafā', and Quṭb al-Dīn al-Shīrāzī, which was widely applied to medicine and its allied health sciences, cognitive science, and the formulation of educational theories, was essentially based on psychological principles and perspectives in the Qur'an. Apart from referring to the three states or stages of development of the human soul mentioned above, the Qur'an outlines its structural and functional components. The Qur'an says: "By the Soul (*nafs*), and the proportion and order given to it, and its enlightenment

---

203. *The Qur'an*, chapter 75 ("The Resurrection"), verse 2. The self-reproaching soul within the human microcosm implies that man is endowed with a faculty of choice, a microcosmic fact that was also implied by God's command toĀdam to "enjoy as you wish but not to approach this tree." The faculty of choice implies that Ādam (peace be upon him!) could transgress the Divine command, which he in fact did, meaning that he has the capacity of evil.

204. *The Qur'an*, chapter 89 ("The Break of Day"), verse 27. *Al-nafs al-muṭma'innah*, which carries the meaning of the tranquil soul or the soul that is in peace, bliss and a state of complete satisfaction, is described in the verse that follows (89:28) as the soul returning "to your Lord well pleased [yourself] (*rāḍiatan*) and well-pleasing unto Him! (*marḍiyatan*)."

205. *The Qur'an*, chapter 12 ("Joseph"), verse 53.

as to its wrong (*fujūr*) and its right (*taqwā*); truly he succeeds that purifies it, and he fails that corrupts it."[206] In the rational and scientific formulation of their psychological theories these philosophers and scientists might have adopted the conceptual tools and terminologies of their pre-Islamic predecessors such as the Greeks, but the basic frameworks of these theories were unmistakably Qur'anic if even if there are assertions to the contrary. A sound understanding of the Qur'an's complete view of the nature, structure, functions, and the various possible states and stages of development of the human soul would be of tremendous help to us to gain a better insight into the meaning of the verses in passages B and C that deal with the subtle and psychic component of the human microcosm.

Both Passages B and C refer to the forbidden tree[207] that symbolizes the prohibited exit door from the state of bliss, innocence, and justice as symbolized by the Garden (*al-jannah*) to the state of *ẓulm*.[208] The Arabic word *ẓulm* conveys a wide

---

206. *The Qur'an*, chapter 91 ("The Sun"), verses 7-10.

207. The Qur'an says, "And do not approach this tree (*wa lā taqrabā hādhihi al-shajarah*)." See chapter 2 ("The Cow"), verse 35; and chapter 7 ("The Heights"), verses 19, 20, and 22. Significantly, Satan did not deny the fact that God has forbidden Ādam (peace be upon him!) to approach the tree, but he deceived him about the true intention of the forbiddance: "Your Lord only forbade you this tree, lest you should become angels or such beings as live forever" (7:20).

208. Asad interprets the forbidden tree as "simply an allegory of the limits which the Creator has set to man's desires and actions: limits beyond which he may not go without offending against his own, God-willed nature." See M. Asad, *The Message of the Qur'an*, note 106, p. 578. This interpretation is plausible, since the Qur'an seems to be referring to the "forbidden tree" as

range of meanings, embracing the ideas of injustice, harm, wrong, transgression, and darkness. The Qur'an uses the word *ẓulm* and its derivatives both in the sense of injustice to oneself and injustice to others. In the former sense, one is understood to have caused disfigurement and disorder to the "naturally" well-ordered space of one's soul that is characterized by proportion (*taswīya*) and balance (*ta'dīl*).[209] Injustice to oneself may then be described as microcosmic in dimension, and it points to disorderliness in the subtle and psychic space of one's microcosmic constitution. Injustice to others, on the other hand, may be said to be macrocosmic in dimension. It is to the microcosmic dimension of *ẓulm* that this verse in Passage C refers when it says: "Our Lord! We have wronged our own souls (*ẓalamnā anfusanā*): if You do not forgive us and do not bestow upon us Your Mercy, we shall certainly be lost."[210] And from the point of view of our interest in pointers in passage C to the existence of a subtle dimension in the human microcosm, it is the microcosmic dimension of *ẓulm* that interests us here more. Pertinently, this verse itself may be counted as one of these pointers.

The expulsion (*khurūj*) of Ādam (peace be upon him!) and Eve[211] through the prohibited exit door upon their tasting of

---

the limit of human behavior that should not be transgressed. Moreover, it does not conflict with any other verse in the Qur'an.

209. The Qur'an, chapter 82 ("The Cleaving Asunder"), verse 7 says: "Him Who created you, then proportioned (*sawwā*) you, then balanced (*'adala*) you ..."

210. *The Qur'an*, chapter 7 ("The Heights"), verse 23.

211. The Qur'an says: "Get them out of the state [of bliss and felicity] in which they had been (*faakhrajahumā min mā kānā fih*)" (2:36).

the forbidden tree is presented in the Qur'an as the descent or fall (*hubūt*) of man,[212] because it was effected from a higher state of human consciousness to its lower state that admits of possible further falls to yet lower and lower states. Scholars of traditional spiritual anthropology and psychology often refer to this lower state of human consciousness to which Ādam (peace be upon him!) had fallen as the domain of the "fallen soul" and quite clearly with justification. It is in its clarification of the expulsion of Ādam (peace be upon him!) and Eve from the Garden and the various dimensions of their fallen state that Passage C provides more detailed information than does passage B about the pointers to the subtle component of the Adamic constitution. For example, Passage B mentions Satan as the cause of Ādam's expulsion and consequential fall but without further explaining them. Passage C provides their explanations as follows.

Satan succeeded in getting Ādam (peace be upon him!) and his wife out of the Garden and leading them (*dallāhumā*) to their fall through deceit (*ghurūr*)[213] in the form of deluding thoughts and arguments in the pretext of giving sincere advice

---

212. The Qur'an says: "Get you down, all [you people], with enmity between yourselves" (*ihbiṭū ba'ḍukum li-ba'ḍ 'aduw*). See chapter 2 ("The Cow"), verse 36; and chapter 7 ("The Heights"), verses 13, and 24. The noun *hubūt*, which may be translated as descent or fall, is etymologically related to the verb *ihbiṭū* used in these verses. The verse 2:36 also refers to the cause of the Fall, namely Satan who "make them [*i.e.* Ādam and Eve] slip [from the Garden] (*fa azallahumā al-shaiṭān 'anhā*)." The verb *azalla*, which is of the fourth form, carries the meaning of causing someone to slip or stumble leading to a fall.

213. The Qur'an says: "So by deceit he brought about their fall ..." (chapter 7, verse 22).

to them.[214] His deceit made the couple slip from the upper "garden floor" of the cosmic edifice through the prohibited exit door only to fall down to the world of *ẓulm* below. It was in the form of a false advice which is the very opposite of the one God has earlier given. In God's advice,[215] the couple were told not to approach and taste the forbidden tree, lest they would become evildoers (*min al-ẓālimīn*). In Satan's advice, on the other hand, which is actually a perverse interpretation of God's advice, the couple were told to understand that God had only forbidden them to taste the tree in question lest they should become angel-like or live an eternal life (7:20). A verse in Passage E provides further clarification of Satan's deceptive advice mentioned in Passage C. It refers to Satan speaking of the tree of immortality or eternal life (*shajarah al-khuld*) on earth and inviting Ādam (peace be upon him!) to join him in approaching the tree.[216] The same verse also speaks of Satan offering to lead Ādam to "a kingdom that never decays (*mulk lā yablā*)."

God's advice is, of course, the right one, since He knows

214. "And he swore to them: "Verily, I am one of your sincere advisors (*min al-nāṣiḥīn*)."" *The Qur'an*, chapter 7, verse 21.

215. The Qur'an summarizes God's original advice and command as follows: [1] Ādam (peace be upon him!) should not approach the "forbidden tree" because to go against this command would result in evil consequences for him; [2] Satan is Ādam's and Eve's avowed enemy (*'adūwun mubīn*); and [3] Ādam (peace be upon him!) and Eve should never allow Satan to get them both out of the Garden as to land themselves in the state of *ẓulm* and misery (*shaqwā*). See *The Qur'an*, chapter 2 ("The Cow"), verse 35; chapter 7 ("The Heights"), verses 19 and 22; chapter 20 ("Ṭā Ḥā"), verse 117.

216. *The Qur'an*, chapter 20 ("Ṭā Ḥā"), verse 120.

perfectly the Adamic reality as well as the reality external to it. Even Satan knows that it is the right advice as evident from his acknowledgment of his powerlessness to mislead God's servants (*'ibād*) who are sincere and purified (*al-mukhliṣīn*) from the straight path.[217] In other words, he knows that he will fail to seduce the sincere servants of God, because they understand the true meaning of the forbidden tree and the evil implications of its tasting. On account of this understanding of theirs and their faith in God, these servants remain obedient to His command. However, as an avowed enemy of Ādam (7:22) and his progeny,[218] Satan promised to assault them from all

---

217. In the following verses in Passage D, Satan vows to mislead Ādam (peace be upon him!) and his descendants: "O my Lord! Because You have put me in the wrong (*aghwaytanī*), I will make [wrong] fair-seeming to them on the earth, and I will put them all in the wrong except Your servants among them who are sincere and purified." *The Qur'an*, chapter 15 ("The Rocky Tract"), verses 39-40.

218. The Qur'an cautions Ādam's progeny (*banī Ādam*) not to be seduced by Satan "in the same manner as he got your parents out of the Garden." They are vulnerable to Satan's seduction and assault, because "he and his tribe (*qabīluhu*) watch you from a position where you cannot see them." See chapter 7 ("The Heights"), verse 27. Commenting on the last part of this verse, Ibn 'Arabī says: "So he [*i.e.* Satan] and his tribe see us with a witnessing of the eyes, and we see him through faith, not with the eyes." William C. Chittick, *The Self-Disclosure of God*, p. 215. In the perspective of the Qur'an, faith and knowledge are not mutually exclusive but are rather inseparable from each other. Faith may be understood as a particular mode of knowing that concerns the exercise of reason. As Ibn al-'Arabī asserts, quoted in Chittick's above work (p. 130), "reason knows what eyesight never witnesses." For a discussion of the essential relationship between faith and knowledge from the epistemological perspective, see Osman Bakar, *Classification of Knowledge in Islam*, chapter 3.

sides[219] to deviate them from God's straight path.[220] Satan succeeded in seducing Ādam (peace be upon him!) to disobey God[221] by taking advantage of the particular moment in Ādam's state of consciousness when he forgot God and His original advice.[222] It was in such a state of consciousness or frame of mind that Ādam (peace be upon him!) was found to be weak and vulnerable to Satan's seduction and deceit.[223] As earlier stated, Satan's deceptive strategy was to offer to lead Ādam (peace be upon him!) to the promised land of immortality, not in the hereafter life (*al-ākhirah*) but in this transient earthly life (*al-dunyā*).

Just to understand what sort of creature he is[224] – clever and

---

219. *The Qur'an*, chapter 7 ("The Heights"), verse 17: "Then I will assault them from before them and behind them, from their right and their left..."

220. *The Qur'an*, chapter 7 ("The Heights"), verse 16: "... I will lie in wait for them on your straight way (*ṣirāt al-mustaqīm*)."

221. The Qur'an, chapter 20 ("Ṭā Ḥa"), verse 121 says: "And so they both [*i.e.* Ādam and Eve] ate of the tree ... and thus did Ādam disobey his Lord and thus did he fall into grievous error." In a verse in Passage C, God told Iblīs in no uncertain terms that "for over My servants no authority shall you have, except such as put themselves in the wrong and follow you," chapter 15 ("The Rocky Tract"), verse 42.

222. Says the Qur'an, chapter 20 ("Ṭā Ḥa"), verse 115: "We had already, beforehand, taken the covenant of Ādam , but he forgot (*nasiya*) ..."

223. "But he forgot and We found on his part no firm resolve," *The Qur'an*, 20:115.

224. The most complete portrayal of Satan in the Qur'an is perhaps found in verses 119 and 120 of chapter 4 ("The Women"): he misleads men, creates in them false desires, encourages idolatrous practices, defaces or corrupts God's creation, and makes deceptive promises.

cunning but mean – and what sort of enemy man has in him, it would be enough to see some of Satan's doings that are only full of contradictions. He promised Ādam immortality on earth when he knew very well that the latter had a mortal dimension, namely a gross physical body (*bashar*) made up of elements from the world of generation and corruption,[225] to which he himself explicitly referred as the reason he refused to bow down to Ādam (peace be upon him!).[226] However, Ādam (peace be upon him!) was promised an unattainable goal, because it was not based upon reality. Rather the goal was an illusory one. Both the ideas of human immortality and eternal kingdom of prosperity on earth are false. Immortality or eternity and earthly life are mutually contradictory ideas, and the more so when this earthly life is conceived in terms of transgressions

---

225. Both God and Satan maintain that Ādam 's body (*bashar*) was created "from sounding clay, from mud molded into shape." Clay is from the world of generation and corruption (*al-kawn wa'l-fasād*). The whole phrase is uttered by God in Passage D of the Qur'an, chapter 15 ("The Rocky Tracts"), verse 29. Satan echoed these words in verse 33 of this chapter. However, God's and Satan's uses of the word *bashar* do not convey the same meaning and significance. In God's usage, *bashar* is only a component of the Adamic constitution. It was the receptacle of the Spirit which God blew into Ādam (peace be upon him!). In Satan's usage, *bashar* is identical to the Adamic reality. In other words, he has reduced the reality of Ādam (peace be upon him!) to his physical body. In this act of reductionism in Satan's thinking we find the prototype of philosophical reductionisms in the history of human thought, especially in the forms we encountered in modern times.

226. In chapter 15, verse 33, the Qur'an presents Iblīs as having replied to God as follows when He asked him why he refused to bow down to Ādam (peace be upon him!): "I am not one to prostrate to *bashar*, whom You created from sounding clay (*ṣalṣāl*), from mud (*ḥama'*) moulded into shape (*masnūn*)."

against the limits imposed by God. The idea of immortality on earth may be false, but Satan has the unsurpassable ability and power to make it appear plausible and sound appealing, especially to the un-alert mind. On the basis of his own testimony in the Qur'an, we know that Satan has the ability to make wrong appear as right and fair, false as true, and bad and evil as seemingly good.[227]

The various ideas that come from Satan as mentioned in Passage C (7:12; 7:16; 7:20), Passage D (15:33; 15:39), and Passage E (20:120) clearly point to his exceptionally good ability at perverting truths and then presenting this perverted truth as if it were truth itself. Satan's idea of immortality is a good example of how he perverts truths to serve some evil purposes. The idea of immortality, understood in its post-humus sense, is of course a truth that is repeatedly affirmed by the Qur'an itself.[228] However, Satan perverted it by transposing its true domain of applicability in eternal time and space to the present transient earthly life. It is this perverted truth of immortality that he presented to Ādam (peace be upon him!) as the real truth.

A point to be borne in mind is that for someone to be seducible by a perverted truth, he must have in his inner nature or in the depth of his soul some form of prior connection to the

---

227. Says Iblīs, "I will make [wrong] fair-seeming to them on the earth (*la'uzaiyinan lahum fi'l-arḍ*) ..." *The Qur'an*, chapter 15 ("The Rocky Tract"), verse 39.

228. In so many of its verses the Qur'an affirms that "those who believe and do righteous deeds" will, in their post-humus life," be admitted to the Garden [*i.e.* the eternal abode of Peace and Prosperity] wherein they will abide forever.

original truth. Since Ādam (peace be upon him!) was created for immortality there must exist in him the innate desire for it. And apparently Satan knew that Ādam (peace be upon him!) had an immortal dimension within his own being and constitution and a desire for immortality. One good argument to support this view is that Satan was commanded by God to acknowledge Ādam's superiority to him – surely on account of the immortal spirit He had blown into him that survives physical death – although Satan deliberately concealed or kept silent about this immortal element in Ādam (peace be upon him!) and instead highlighted the latter's mortal *bashar* so that he could advance his claim of superiority over him and thereby disobey the Divine command that he bowed down to him.

So we find Satan in one moment highlighting immortality so that his deceit prevailed and yet in another moment concealing it out of arrogance so that his egoism might be served. He cleverly exploited Ādam's desire for immortality, albeit misdirecting it to serve his evil design. His hidden agenda was to seduce Ādam into viewing the forbidden tree not as the tree of good and evil that he should prohibit himself from tasting but as the tree of eternal life that is to be tasted, thereby removing the obstacle to his plan to take Ādam (peace be upon him!) out of the Garden and lead him into the world of *ẓulm* and *shaqwā*.

The idea of immortality is a particular dimension of the more general idea of a "better life" that is yet to come. It concerns the human future with which every human being is excited about. So Satan sought to also arouse the desire in Ādam (peace be upon him!) for a better life that could be in store for him. In Passage E, the verses 20:118-119 describe the "life of sufficiency" in the "Kingdom" of the Garden that God has provided for the Adamic species in the following terms: "There is therein [enough provision] for you not to go hungry nor to go naked, nor to suffer from thirst, nor from the sun's heat." It was upon God telling Ādam (peace be upon him!) of the good life on earth He has made available for him and his progeny as mentioned in this verse that Satan countered with an offer of a better life, which was symbolized, in his own words, by "the tree of eternal life and the kingdom that never decays (20:120)."In other words, Satan promised Ādam (peace be upon him!) immortality and the eternal kingdom of peace and prosperity.

By itself, Satan's seductive power could not have made Ādam (peace be upon him!) disobey God (*'aṣā Ādam rabbahu*). Ādam's state of mind or consciousness must also have an important role to play in his succumb to Satan's temptation and deceit. We are referring to his state of heedlessness (*ghafla*) and forgetfulness (*nisyān*). Significantly, in Passage E, the references to Satan's evil suggestion (20:120) and Ādam's disobedience of God's prohibition (20:121) are preceded by the reference to Ādam's forgetfulness (20:115), implying that there was a causal relation between his forgetfulness and Satan's seduction. Thus the majority of the Qur'an's interpreters (*mufaṣṣirūn*), both classical and modern, understand Ādam's forgetfulness as conveying the specific meaning of a particular Divine command or a particular obligation God had earlier enjoined on him that he has forgotten.[229] According to their

229. *Tafsīr ibn 'Abbās* (p. 347) interprets the Arabic *fa nasiya* as "he left what he was commanded to do." Among modern translators of the Qur'an in the English language, we have, for example, Muhammad Asad rendering *fa nasiya* as "but he forgot it" whereas Yusuf 'Ali and the translator of *Tafsīr ibn 'Abbās* (p. 347) render it as simply "but he forgot," without the object of

interpretation, the knowledge from God that Ādam (peace be upon him!) has forgotten is mentioned in the verses 20:117-119. In essence, Ādam (peace be upon him!) forgot God's forewarning to him that Satan was an enemy to him and his wife, who would do every dirty trick imaginable to get them out of the Garden into the world of misery. Ādam (peace be upon him!) also forgot God's assurance to him that all his needs could be met in the Garden without him having to venture outside it.

From the philosophical and psychological perspectives, Ibn al-'Arabī offers a very profound interpretation of Ādam's forgetfulness, which however represents a minority view among the classical interpreters and, in fact, even until now. In this interpretation he explains that forgetfulness (*nisyān*) and heedlessness (*ghafla*) are necessary components of human nature created by God in that these psychological elements are to contribute to man's ultimate goal of becoming the perfect man (*al-insān al-kāmil*). Ibn al-'Arabī quotes the following Prophetic hadith in providing the traditional foundational

---

the verb "forgot" mentioned, which we maintain, linguistically speaking, is the more correct one, leaving it as it were to the interpreters to interpret what was exactly that Ādam (peace be upon him!) forgot. In his interpretation Asad explains what the "it" that Ādam forgot refers to. However, in quoting the authority of Fakhr al-Dīn al-Rāzī, Asad also notes that although the thing forgotten may be specific, the message of the story of Ādam's forgetfulness is universal. The message is that "negligence of spiritual truths is one of the recurrent characteristics of the human race, which is symbolized by Ādam." See M. Asad, *The Message of the Qur'an*, p. 577, note 102. Yusuf 'Ali does not provide any direct commentary on Ādam's forgetfulness but he just points to his "little firmness" in resisting Satan's temptation to the point of succumbing to it. See his *The Meaning of the Holy Qur'an*, p. 651, note 2640.

support for the view that the human being is naturally disposed to forgetfulness: "Ādam forgot, so his offspring forgot."[230] Ibn al-'Arabī also came up with a compelling definition and characterization of the prototype of forgetfulness that befell the first human being, namely Ādam (peace be upon him!). He describes forgetfulness and heedlessness generally as both "states that overtake the human configuration," and he adds that "states have a property in absolutely everything qualified by *wujūd*."[231]

As argued by Ibn al-'Arabī, one property or form of the state of forgetfulness is the imagination of the forgetters "that they have a portion of lordship or that God has appointed a share of it for them."[232] In other words, the imagination of the forgetter is such that *tawḥīd* is compromised. There are many ways in which *tawḥīd* could be compromised. Ibn al-'Arabī deduced the above property or characterization of forgetfulness from the verse of the Qur'an concerning the forgetting of God by the hypocrites. Says the verse: "They forgot God, so He forgot them."[233] This form of forgetfulness is, however, deliberate and active and not "involuntary" or passive in nature. It depicts a deliberate turning away from God's decree on good and evil in favor of doing the opposite, namely "enjoining evil and forbidding what are just" (9:67). In the case of the original forgetfulness of Ādam (peace be upon him!), its property or form was rather "involuntary" or passive in nature

230. William C. Chittick, *The Self-Disclosure of God*, p. 323.

231. William C. Chittick, *The Self-Disclosure of God*, p. 77.

232. William C. Chittick, *The Self-Disclosure of God*, p. 199.

233. *The Qur'an*, chapter 9 ("The Repentance"), verse 67.

as implied by its characterization as an effect of Satan's seduction.

Ādam's state of heedlessness and forgetfulness was one in which he "acts freely in it[234] through his own self, this free acting by himself dismisses the Real from trusteeship."[235] Free will and faculty of choice were Ādam's rights (sing: *ḥaqq*), but God is the trustee (*wakīl*) of them.[236] By transgressing against His order not to taste the forbidden tree with the desire to attain immortality and eternity independently of God, Ādam (peace be upon him!) removed in his thought God's position as the sole trustee. There was a movement within Ādam's consciousness from the state of mind in which he always took God as his sole trustee to the state of mind in which he saw himself as the trustee of what he owned and what he did, viewing himself as self-sufficient.[237] Ibn al-'Arabī appears to be

---

234. In Chittick's translation of Ibn al-'Arabī's passage, the pronoun 'it' refers to any movement of the forgetter in which the forgetter is heedless. See *The Self-Disclosure of God*, p. 77. Since we are applying the passage to help explain Ādam's state of forgetfulness, the pronoun 'it' refers to his movement toward the tree of immortality and the kingdom of eternal sustainability.

235. William C. Chittick, *The Self-Disclosure of God*, p. 77.

236. Ibn al-'Arabī cites the verse 9, chapter 73 ("The Enwrapped One") to emphasize the Divine trusteeship of man's rights and *tawḥīd* as the core idea that sustains man's acceptance of this trusteeship in his life and thought. The verse says: "Lord of the east and the west, there is no god but He, so take Him as a trustee (*wakīl*)." For Ibn al-'Arabī's commentary on this verse, see William C. Chittick, *The Self-Disclosure of God*, p. 77.

237. According to the Qur'an, man by nature tends to transgress and view himself as self-sufficient. It says: "Nay, but man transgresses all bounds, in that he looks upon himself as self-sufficient." See chapter 96 ("The Clinging

identifying Ādam's original forgetfulness with this latter state of mind in which he dismissed God from trusteeship. It is in the sense of this latter state of consciousness that Ādam (peace be upon him!) may be said to have forgotten God.

Ibn al-'Arabī introduced the concept of "circular trusteeship," which he says is derived from the verse "Lord of the east and the west, there is no god but He, so take him as a trustee" (73:9). He explains that, in accordance with the reality of *tawḥīd* as emphasized in this verse, God's trusteeship is necessarily "absolute, authorized, and circular." By "circular trusteeship," he means that whenever man dismisses God from trusteeship, He is only to appear again to take charge of his affairs."[238] God's solicitude to His servants is what makes His trusteeship necessarily circular. Thus we find that after the spiritual fall of Ādam (peace be upon him!) and his wife that landed them in a state of *ẓulm* it was God who called on them (*nādāhumā*) to refresh their mind about His original directive that they have forgotten.[239] They responded to His call by admitting their great mistake and pleading for His Mercy so that they might return to their original state of remembrance.

The important point to be noted is that it was not until God

---

Clot"), verses 6-7. These negative dispositions in human nature are traceable in origin to Ādam's constitution itself, since in his spiritual history Ādam (peace be upon him!) went through the experience of committing transgression against a Divine command and acting freely independently of God as if he were self-sufficient.

238. William C. Chittick, *The Self-Disclosure of God*, p. 77.

239. *The Qur'an*, chapter 7 ("The Heights"), verse 22: "And their Lord called on them: "Did I not forbid you that tree, and tell you that Satan was an avowed enemy unto you?""

has given the forgetter mercy from Him that he was able to return to his former state of remembrance or recollection. The same truth is conveyed in verse 20:122 but expressed differently where it is said that when Ādam (peace be upon him!) went astray (*ghawā*) following his disobedience of God, "his Lord chose (*ajtabā*) him [for His Grace]: He turned to him (*tāba 'alaihi*) and gave him guidance (*hadā*)." In so doing, God is asserting His trusteeship again, this time as "Lord of the west" in which context Ādam's movement was guided back to what Ibn al-'Arabī refers to as the "non-manifest domain." Ādam (peace be upon him!) went astray in the manifest domain, as symbolized by the spatial direction of "the east," in the illusive quest for immortality and eternity, because he dismissed the trusteeship of "Lord of the east."

It is clear from the foregoing discussion of Ādam's spiritual fall and the various issues that are closely intertwined with it – such as Satan's seduction and deceit, his original forgetfulness and tasting of the forbidden tree and his straying into the world "outside of God" – that the verses of the Qur'an dealing with them provide a wealth of information about the spiritual, subtle, and imaginal dimension of Ādam's microcosmic reality. The story of Ādam's spiritual fall as found in the Qur'an is basically the story of an exploration into the psychological space of human consciousness that constitutes a very important part of the human microcosm, particularly its subtle and psychic dimension.

## The Idea of the Microcosm in the Chapter of the Rocky Tract (Passage D)

In the course of discussing Passage C in the last section with the stated aim of further explaining, clarifying, and complementing Passage B in the understanding of the Adamic reality and constitution, we have made many references to verses in passages D and E, since these verses provide additional insights into the discussion. Nonetheless, especially for the benefit of readers who are not in a position to directly consult the Qur'an, we reproduce below the whole of Passage D taken from the chapter of the rocky tract (*al-ḥijr*) so that they may compare and contrast it with Passages B and C to see their subtle differences in approaches to and perspectives on the same issues despite their outward resemblance in linguistic expressions. Passage D reads as follows:

> We created man (*insān*) from sounding clay (*ṣalṣāl*), from mud molded into shape (*ḥama' masnūn*) (15:26);
>
> And the jinn race (*al-jann*), We had created before, from the fire of a scorching wind (*nār al-samūm*) (15:27).
>
> Behold! Your Lord said to the angels: "I am about to create man (*bashar*), from sounding clay from mud molded into shape" (15:28);
>
> "When I have fashioned him (in due proportion) (*sawwaytuhu*) and breathed into him (*nafakhtu fīhī*) of My spirit (*rūḥī*), fall you down in obeisance unto him" (15:29).
>
> So the angels prostrated themselves, all of them together (15:30):
>
> Not so Iblīs: he refused to be among those who prostrated themselves (15:31).
>
> God said: "O Iblīs! What is your reason for not being among those who prostrated themselves?" (15:32)

[Iblīs] said: "I am not one to prostrate myself to man (*bashar*), whom You created from sounding clay, from mud molded into shape" (15:33).

[God] said: "Then get you out from here; for you are rejected, accursed (*rajīm*) (15:34).

"And the curse shall be on you till the Day of Judgment" (15:35).

[Iblīs] said: "O my Lord! Give me then respite till the Day the [dead] are raised" (15:36).

[God] said: "Respite is granted to you till the Day of the Time Appointed (*al-waqt al-ma'lūm*)" (15:37-38).

[Iblīs] said: "O my Lord! Because You have put me in the wrong, I will make [wrong] fair-seeming (*'uzayyinan*) to them on the earth, and I will put them all in the wrong (15:39).

"Except the sincere and purified (*al-mukhliṣīn*) among Your servants" (15:40).

[God] said: "This [way of My sincere servants] is indeed a way that leads straight to Me (15:41).

"For over My servants no authority shall you have, except such as put themselves in the wrong and follow you" (15:42).

And verily, Hell is the promised abode for them all! (15:43)

In affirming the idea of man as a microcosm, the above Passage D complements Passages B and C in several ways. It refers to the structure and the total dimensions of the human constitution in a more explicit way. Passages B and C describe

Ādam (peace be upon him!) as a person, as the first man, the first husband, the first ancestor of the human species, and implicitly as the first Prophet of God. Passage D, however, does not mention Ādam (peace be upon him!) by name, although its verses clearly apply to him as shown by similarly sounding verses in Passages B and C. Its main concern is with the human species as a whole that descended from Ādam (peace be upon him!) and his wife. Thus it speaks of *insān* – man as such, not a particular human being – a term not found in Passages B and C. Quite clearly, particularly through its verses 15:28-29, Passage D depicts man (*insān*) as a microcosm in broad structural terms that are more concrete and detailed than what we find in Passages B and C.

Passage B does not at all speak of Ādam's form; Passage C does so but it merely mentions Ādam (peace be upon him!) as being given shape and form (*ṣūra*) (7:11) without explaining and detailing it. In contrast, Passage D presents the complete man (*insān*) as having three fundamental component forms, namely a material or physical form as indicated by the phrase "from sounding clay, from mud molded into shape," (15:26 and 15:28), a spiritual form as indicated by the phrase "blew into him of My spirit," (15:29) and an "intermediate form" (*barzakh*) the existence of which, however, is only implied in the passage. The "intermediate" form refers to the soul (*nafs*),[240] which becomes manifest "between the divine inblowing and the proportioned body."[241] The verse (15:29) "when I have

240. This refers to the human soul that is ranked higher than the animal soul and 'envelops' the latter.

241. William C. Chittick, *The Self-Disclosure of God*, p. 271. In explaining this occasion of the manifestation of the soul in the human body in the

proportioned him and blown into him of My spirit" is the one in passage C that alludes to the "intermediate" form. *Insān* comes into existence between the Divine act of proportioning the body in a state of preparedness (*isti'dād*) as indicated by the phrase *sawwaytuhu* ("I have proportioned him") and the Divine act of breathing something of His spirit into the body as indicated by the phrase *wa*[242] *nafakhtu fīhī min rūḥīy* ("and I

---

process of reproductive creation of *insān*, Ibn al-'Arabī quotes the verse 9, chapter 32 ("The Prostration"), which is similar in meaning to the verse 15:29. It is to be noted, however, that the verse 9:32 refers to God in the third person, whereas the reference to Him in the verse 15:29 is made in the first person.

242. Even the conjunction '*wa*' constituted of a single letter '*waw*', here translated as 'and' becomes significant in the understanding of the sequential order of the two Divine acts, which also possesses a scientific dimension. The conjunction 'and' in the verse may be interpreted as denoting concomitance, that is, as meaning occurring together or simultaneously. See Edward W. Lane, *Arabic-English Lexicon*, vol. 2, p. 3048. Although in the verse both *taswīya* ("proportioning") arising from the verb *sawwa* and *nafakh* ("blowing") arising from the verb *nafakha* refer to God's acts, we may speak of one act as of being prior in principle, not in time, to the other. In one sense, the proportioning of the body is prior to the breathing of the Divine Spirit into the body, since the proportioned body is to serve as a receptacle for the spirit that is to be blown into it. In another, the blowing of something of the Divine Spirit into the body has priority over its proportioning, since what is to be blown determines the nature of the receptacle that is to receive the blown object. However, in relation to the creation of *insān*, both acts are in need of each other, and as argued by Ibn al-'Arabī, both also influence each other. There is no "time gap" in the quantitative sense between the two acts, because these acts do not constitute a relative order or sequence. Rather, they occur together and simultaneously. For Ibn al-'Arabī's detailed discussion of the mutual

influence of the body's constitution and the soul on each other, see William C. Chittick, *The Self-Disclosure of God*, pp. 322-329.

The proportioning of man's body and soul, which pertains to form and structure, can only reach its completion with the complete manifestation of the blown spirit in his *bashar* and its permeation of the whole of it. Prior to the blowing of the Divine Spirit into the proportioned body the latter is still without a distinctively human dimension, for it is the former that endows the Adamic form to the proportioned body. *Insān* is yet to be created. So the best body that could be fashioned and proportioned out of existing forms to serve as a receptacle of the blown spirit would only be constituted of physical and subtle elements, the existence of which before man is acknowledged by the verse 15:27. It could serve as the material and subtle basis for the reception of the blown spirit upon which the Adamic human form becomes manifest. The human soul manifested by the blown spirit serves as the transcendent cause to effect the transformation of the "animal form" into the Adamic form. The Qur'an, chapter 23 ("The Believers"), verse 14, seems to be referring to this type of transcendent bodily transformation in reproductive biology when it says that "We made out of that lump bones and clothed the bones with flesh; then We developed out of it another creature (*ansha'nāhu khalqan ākhar*)." This verse refers to a bodily transformation from an animal form to a human form.

Ibn 'Abbās (may God be pleased with him!) interpreted "when I have proportioned him" to mean that "when I created his hands, legs, eyes, and the rest of him" and "and breathed into him of My Spirit" to mean "and place the spirit into him." See *Tafsīr ibn 'Abbās*, p. 275. Since he did not give any other explanation of the two phrases, we may understand his interpretation in two different ways. If we read his usage of the conjunction 'and' in a concomitant sense, then his interpretation of the two phrases may be harmonized with the interpretation we have presented above on the basis of our reading of Ibn al-'Arabī. However, if we read it as implying that there is a strict sequential order between the two acts – the breathing of the Divine Spirit follows exactly after the completion of the proportioning of the body – then we will be confronted with a situation in which a distinctively human body exists when its corresponding human soul is not breathed into him of My spirit"). Only then in the same verse comes the Divine command to bow down to man ("*fa qaʿū lahu sājidīn*"). In other words, as previously affirmed, the bowing down to *insān* that was commanded on the angels – and by extension, all creatures – was with the view of acknowledging the mystery of the Divine spirit in him and the superiority of this spirit over all created forms, including the angelic ones.

The fashioning and proportioning (*taswīya*) of man by God in person, as attested by His reference to Himself in the first pronoun 'I' (15:28-29) and His own words "with My own hands

---

yet within the body. It is like we are saying that we have a living human body with only an animal soul! Since we subscribe to the principle that the human body and the human soul are inseparable and that one implies the other, we go for the first reading of Ibn ʿAbbās that would harmonize with our earlier interpretation.

The idea of identifying the coming into existence of a fully developed human fetus with its ensoulment finds accord with Islamic Law (*Sharīʿah*). While biomedical science can tell us almost with precision the length of time taken by the fetus in the mother's womb to develop into a full human form, we have no knowledge of "how long" the Divine creation of Ādam 's complete human form with all its physical parts lasted to completion. As for the timing of the ensoulment of the body, both in the case of the special creation of Ādam (peace be upon him!) and in the case of the creation of his progeny through the regulated and repeated process of embryological growth, only religious tradition could tell us when it happens. The ensoulment of the body that results from the inblowing of God's Spirit into it happens no sooner than the human form is completed. This knowledge based on tradition enables Islamic law to apply it to several areas of legal and ethical-moral concern such as abortion. However, as if to emphasize the imperfection of the physical and human worlds in which we live, God draws the attention of man to exceptional irregularities in human embryology.

(*khalaqtu bi-yadayy*)"[243] in reference to His creation of Ādam (peace be upon him!), pertains to both the physical form and the "intermediate form" which may be described as the animal form. The animal form concerns the biological and subtle worlds. Passage D alludes to the three stages of God's creation of *insān* corresponding to the three component forms of man just mentioned. The first two stages refer to the creation of *bashar*, a term attributed in the passage to God Himself and which is not found in the earlier two passages.[244] God describes the *bashar* that He intends to create as being formed out of a physical substance called "sounding clay (*ṣalṣāl*)," which is itself formed from "mud (*ḥama'*) molded into shape (*masnūn*)" and which is to be further fashioned and proportioned. The sounding clay (*ṣalṣāl*)[245] is to serve as the material basis for the

243. This phrase is found in Passage G. The Qur'an says: "O Iblīs! What prevents you from prostrating yourself to one whom I have created with My hands?" Chapter 38 ("Ṣād"), verse 75. These verses (15:28-29 and 38:75) provide clear scriptural proof that the first man was specially created by God and that he did not evolve from lower animal forms through a long natural process of biological evolution as maintained in modern biology. This fundamental thesis of the Qur'an on the origin of the human species has by no means been disproved by modern biology or any other branch of modern science despite claims to the contrary. See Osman Bakar, ed., *Critique of Evolutionary Theory* (Kuala Lumpur: Islamic Academy of Science, 1987).

244. A more detailed explanation of the meaning of *bashar* is to follow later.

245. The word *ṣalṣāl* occurs four times in the Qur'an, thrice in this Passage D under discussion (15:26; 15:28; 15:33) and once in chapter 55 ("The Most Gracious"), verse 14. According to most philologists, the word means "dry clay that emits, when touched, a sound like pottery." Both Yusuf 'Ali and Asad understand this meaning as alluding to man's power of speech. See Abdullah Yusuf 'Ali, *The Meaning of the Holy Qur'an*, p. 513, note 1966;

second stage of the creation of *bashar* which involves the transcendental process[246] of fashioning and proportioning hierarchic layers of non-physical, living forms within the human body[247] that are identifiable with the world of subtle life

---

Muhammad Asad, *The Message of the Qur'an*, p, 416, note 24. Asad writes: "... since it [*i.e. ṣalṣāl*] is used in the Qur'an exclusively with reference to the creation of man, it seems to contain an allusion to the power of *articulate speech* which distinguishes man from all other animal species, as well as to the brittleness of his existence" (p. 416).

246. The process of *taswīya* is transcendental in nature, because God personally actualized and completed the process as made clear by the phrase "I have proportioned him" (*sawwaytuhu*).

247. In the Qur'an, the idea of Divine proportioning of man is also applied to his non-physical parts, namely to his subtle body and psychological constitution. The form II verb, *sawwa*, which carries among others the basic meanings of "to make something symmetrical, complete, congruous or consistent in its parts, and adaptive to its exigencies, and to fashion and proportion with the view of securing order and perfection," occurs 13 times in the Qur'an. For a philological understanding of the usage of the verb in these verses of the Qur'an, see Edward W. Lane, *Arabic-English Lexicon*, vol. 1, pp. 1476-1477. Although in all these occurrences the verb in its various forms is associated with the Divine activity of fashioning and proportioning with the view of realizing order and perfection, it is not in all of them that the activity pertains to the human constitution. However, it is quite clear that whenever the activity pertains to the constituents of man it is not limited to just the physical ones. The verse 91:7, for example, applies the divine proportioning of man to his psychological constitution: "By the soul (*nafs*) and the proportion and order [He] gave to it." Other verses conveying the idea of a comprehensive proportioning of man that goes beyond his physical components include 18:37 and 82:7. On the basis of these verses, it is possible to interpret the divine *taswīya* in verse 15:29 as embracing the proportioning of man's cellular constitution studied by microbiology and his psychological constitution studied by psychology.

forms, intelligence, and consciousness. This subtle world is symbolized by the jinn species (*al-jann*) of which Iblīs or Satan is a notorious member.[248] The significance of this species being mentioned in passing as having been created before the human species (15:27), right after God made known His intention to create *insān*, is to highlight the fact that the jinn species as a whole[249] has a role to play in the creation of man's *bashar*.

The divine *taswīya* of man's *bashar* is meant to prepare for the third and final stage of the creation of *insān*, namely the blowing of something of the Divine Spirit into the *bashar* thus prepared to receive it. *Insān*, the complete and real man, thus comprises *bashar* and the breathed part of the Divine Spirit that has become differentiated, particularized, and individualized as a result of its reception by the *bashar*. In each living *insān*, there is what Ibn al-'Arabī called a differentiated particular spirit (*rūḥ juz'ī*) born of the undifferentiated Divine

248. In the chapter of "the Jinn" (chapter 72), the Qur'an informs us that, like the human species, the jinn species may be broadly classified into two groups: [1] the believers (*al-mu'minūn*) in God (72:2), the righteous (*al-ṣāliḥūn*) (72:11), and the submitters to God's Will (*al-muslimūn*) (72:14); and [2] the opposites of the first group. However, on the testimony of a group of jinns before the Prophet Muḥammad (salutation and peace be upon him!), members of the species "follow divergent paths (*ṭarā'iq qidada*) (72:11). The jinn species inhabit the so-called subtle and hidden world, because they are created from "the fire of a scorching wind (*nār al-samūm*)" (15:27). The subtle world is therefore one in which good and evil freely intermingle as well as clash with each other, since they seek to assert their respective domains of authority and influence.

249. We are arguing that the macrocosmic reality of the jinn species in which we find both good and evil tendencies has microcosmic implications for the structural components of man's *bashar*.

Spirit which he also called "the Universal Spirit" (*al-rūḥ al-kullī*)[250] as a result of its differentiation and particularization as dictated by the state of preparedness (*isti'dād*) of the body, which varies from one person to another. Man's rational soul with all its powers or faculties becomes manifest upon the undifferentiated Divine Spirit's entry into and permeation of his *bashar*. From the scientific perspective of classical Muslim philosophers the whole of the traces of the blowing of something of the Divine Spirit into man's *bashar* is what constitutes the entire space of the human soul with all its powers or faculties. Thus in one verse in Passage F, the breathing into the proportioned body of something of the Divine Spirit is mentioned together with the differentiation of the cognitive power inherent or configured in the Universal Spirit into its constituent parts, the most fundamental of which are the faculties of hearing (*al-sam'*), sight (*al-abṣār*), and understanding (*al-af'idah*).[251]

In our interpretation, following that of Ibn al-'Arabī, which is also in agreement with the view of the Muslim philosopher-scientists such as Ibn Sīnā, the differentiation and particularization of the five physical senses in their distinctively human forms in the development of the fetus do not occur prior to the Divine blowing but rather upon it.[252] It is the

250. William C. Chittick, *The Self-Disclosure of God*, p. 272.

251. *The Qur'an*, chapter 32 ("The Prostration"), verse 9.

252. Our interpretation differs from that of Yusuf 'Ali. He speaks of the four main stages of the reproduction of *insān*. The first stage is that of clay (*ṭīn*) (32:7) serving as the material basis of life. The second stage is that of the creation of sperm – a quintessence of fluid that is despised (*sulālatin min ma'in mahīn*) (32:8) – as the first form of life. The third stage is that of

"fashioning and proportioning" (32:9) of the individual life that comes into existence in consequence of the fertilization of the ovum by the sperm until an animal form of life comes into being. The fourth stage is that of "distinctive man into whom God's spirit is breathed" (32:9) when he rises higher than animals. Yusuf 'Ali is of the view that man gets his five physical [animal] senses in the third stage, that is, prior to the breathing of something of the Divine Spirit into the body. He thinks that man's physical cognitive faculties are developed in the third stage, while the spiritual counterparts of hearing [*i.e.* capacity to hear God's message], seeing [*i.e.* the inner vision], and feeling and understanding [*i.e.* feeling the nobler heights of love and understanding the bearings of inner life] are developed in the fourth and final stage. See Abdullah Yusuf 'Ali, *The Meaning of the Holy Qur'an*, p. 870, notes 3637-3640.

Our response to his view is that the five physical senses are parts of the faculties of the rational soul, but this soul does not become manifest in the body until upon God's blowing something of His Spirit into it. Yusuf 'Ali is correct in maintaining that the formation of the five physical senses is included in the process of *taswīya* [*i.e.* his third stage] but he is wrong in maintaining that these five senses are already a finished product by the time God acts to blow of His Spirit into the body. There is apparently a subtle issue involved here. The issue boils down to what we have discussed in quite details in an earlier note of ours (see note 55 of this chapter), namely the issue of what we call "time gap" and what Asad calls "lapse of time." The issue of time gap does not arise in our interpretation since the coming into being of the human bodily form is concurrent with the blowing of the Divine Spirit. Asad also argues for absence of lapse of time between the proportioning of the body and the blowing of the Divine Spirit but by appealing to the instantaneous nature of the Divine act as implied by the Divine creative command *kun fayakūn*. See Muhammad Asad, *The Message of the Qur'an*, p. 462, note 26. In our case, we rest our argument on one of the fundamental principles of psychology itself. This way we are also bringing a scientific dimension to the discussion of the issues in question, which is an appropriate thing to do, since the issue of being human is partly scientific and partly philosophical-theological in nature.

particular spirit (*al-rūḥ al-juz'ī*) that manifests the forms of human cognition, both physical and non-physical (32:9), which are superior to cognitive forms in the other animals. Nothing that is recognizably human could be in place except upon the particular spirit becoming manifest in the "body" that is undergoing the process of *taswīya*. Muslim philosopher-scientists referred to each manifested human form of cognitive power or human capacity for cognition, including the capacity for articulate speech, as being in a state of potentiality (*bi'l-quwwa*). Human growth and development in their various stages and phases, at least in their knowledge dimension, are essentially about the progressive actualization of this cognitive power in potentiality.

The above discussion of Passage D shows that, details aside, this passage has provided adequate information, explicit and implied, about the fundamental structural components of the Adamic constitution to point to the microcosmic reality of man. In comprising *bashar*, itself constituted of physical and subtle elements, and an inblown spirit that becomes manifest as human soul, the reality of man (*insān*) encompasses the entire dimensions of the microcosm. Further, Iblīs was alluding to a component of man that has the potential or capacity to do evil when he told God that he "will make [wrong] fair-seeming to them [*i.e.* mankind] on the earth," and he "will put them all in the wrong" except the sincere and the purified (15:39-40). The existence of this capacity for evil as a component of the human constitution is confirmed by verses 8-10, chapter 91 ("The Sun"): "And its [*i.e.* the soul's] enlightenment as to its wrong and its right – truly he succeeds that purifies it, and he fails that corrupts it." This verse affirms the existence of evil tendencies within man as a part of his nature that is alluded to in verse

15:39. When actualized, man's evil tendencies partake the nature and characteristics of Iblīs or Satan. In other words, there is a counterpart of Iblīs or Satan in man's microcosmic constitution. The verse also clarifies Iblīs' statement that he is unable to put in the wrong the purifier of his [lower] soul, but he is able to do so in the case of the corruptor of his soul. As a whole, the Passage D provides a clearer picture of the human microcosm when compared to Passages B and C.

**The Idea of Microcosm in the Chapter of Ṭā Ḥā (Passage E)**

We now intend to follow up this discussion with another, albeit a relatively brief one, namely a discussion of Passage E contained in the chapter of *Ṭā Ḥā*. Since a considerable part of this passage has been cited to help clarify issues in the course of our discussion of Passages B, C, and D we will only highlight the part of its content that needs further clarification with the view of arriving at a yet even clearer picture of the microcosm. Passage E reads as follows:

> We had already, beforehand, taken the covenant of Ādam, but he forgot: and We found on his part no firm resolve (20:115)
>
> When We said to the angels, "Prostrate yourselves to Ādam," they prostrated themselves, but not Iblīs: he refused (20:116).
>
> Then We said: "O Ādam! Verily, this is an enemy to you and your wife: so do not let him to get you both out of the Garden, so that you are landed in misery (20:117).
>
> "There is therein [enough provision] for you not to go hungry nor to go naked, nor to suffer from thirst, nor from the sun's heat" (20:118-119).

> But Satan whispered evil to him: he said, "O Ādam! Shall I lead you to the Tree of Eternity and to a kingdom that never decays?" (20:120).
>
> In the result, they both ate of the tree, and so their nakedness appeared to them: they began to sew together, for their covering, leaves from the Garden: thus did Ādam disobey his Lord and become astray (20:121).
>
> But his Lord chose him [for His grace]: He turned to him, and gave him guidance (20:122).
>
> He said: "Get you down, both of you – all together, from the Garden, with enmity one to another: but if, as is sure, there comes to you guidance from Me, whosoever follows My guidance, will not lose his way, nor fall into misery (20:123).
>
> "But whosoever turns away from My message, verily for him is a life narrowed down, and We shall raise him up blind on the Day of Judgment" (20:124).

The above passage mentions several key elements in Ādam's microcosmic space. First, there is the element of forgetfulness (*nisyān*) that played such a fateful role in his spiritual history. The Prophet's saying that Ādam's progeny inherited his forgetfulness clearly means that it is an integral and permanent element of human nature that does not undergo any evolutionary change with the passage of time. So fateful was the role of forgetfulness in Ādam's spiritual fall and so fundamental is its place and role in human nature and man's quest for God that man is called *insān* in Arabic, because the word means "one who forgets." The Adamic species may be described as the forgetful species.

The second element pertains to animal desires – such as the

desire for food, drinks, and clothes – an important part of Ādam's nature, all of which could be fulfilled in the confines of the Garden as promised to him by God but within bounds (20:118-119). The third element pertains to the psychological states of the human condition, both in the positive and negative senses. In the negative sense, this psychological state is indicated by the reference to misery (*tashqā*) (20:117 and 20:123), a straitened and suffocated life (*ma'īshat ḍank*) (20:124), shamefulness (*saw'āt*) (20:121), and a straying mind that has lost direction in its wandering (*ghawā*) (20:121). In the positive sense, the reference is to the state of self-satisfaction as opposed to the feeling of unfulfilled desires, as implied by the verses 20:118-119, and the consciousness of being guided on the right track in life, as implied by the verse 20:123. The seeds of both psychological states are implanted in Ādam's soul. Satan is interested in causing the "negative seeds" to sprout and grow into a tree of evil, while God is interested in seeing them sprouting and growing into a tree of good.

In this Passage E, Satan seeks to lure and seduce Ādam (peace be upon him!) into tasting and experiencing these negative psychological states by disguising them as the fruits of immortality and the eternal kingdom of prosperity. After Ādam (peace be upon him!) was deceived and he tasted the bitter fruits of the tree of evil, God in His Grace and Mercy guided him and his wife back upon the straight path (20:122). God turned to Ādam's innate capacity for goodness and guidance contained within the seeds of "positive" or healthy psychological states implanted in his nature when He wanted to restore him to his state of being prior to his fall. The whole of Passage E does not deal at all with the physical dimension of the microcosm save the sole reference to Ādam's bodily needs.

Its focus is on the spiritual and psychological dimensions and subtle elements of Ādam's constitution.

### The Idea of Microcosm in the Chapter of *Ṣād* (Passage G)

We turn next in this section to Passage G contained in the chapter of *Ṣād*, skipping momentarily Passage F for the reason that we wish to discuss it together with Passage H. We see Passage F as extremely useful in helping to clarify Passage H. Passage G reads as follows:

> Behold, your Lord said to the angels: "I am about to create man (*khāliqun bashar*) from clay (*ṭīn*) (38:71).
>
> "When I have fashioned and proportioned (*sawwaytu*) him and breathed (*nafakhtu*) into him of My spirit, fall you down in obeisance unto him" (38:72).
>
> So the angels prostrated themselves, all of them together (38:73):
>
> Not so Iblīs: he was haughty, and became one of those who reject faith (38:74).
>
> [God] said: "O Iblīs! What prevents you from prostrating yourself to one whom I have created with My hands (*khalaqtu bi-yaday*)? Are you haughty? Or are you one of the high [and mighty] ones?" (38:75)
>
> [Iblīs] said: "I am better than he: You created me from fire (*nār*), and him You created from clay (*ṭīn*)" (38:76).
>
> [God] said: "Then get you out from here: for you are rejected, accursed (*rajīm*) (38:77).
>
> "And my curse (*la'natī*) shall be on you till the Day of Judgment (*yawm al-dīn*)" (38:78).

> [Iblīs] said: "O my Lord! Give me then respite till the Day the [dead] are resurrected (*yawm yubʿathūn*)" (38:79).
>
> [God] said: "Respite then is granted you – till the Day of the Time Appointed (*yawm al-waqt al-maʿlūm*)" (38:80-81).
>
> [Iblīs] said: "Then, by Your power, I will put them all in the wrong, except Your servants amongst them, the sincere and the purified [by Your Grace]" (38:82-83).
>
> [God] said: "Then it is just and fitting (*fa'l-ḥaqq*) – and I say what is just and fitting (*wa'l-ḥaqq aqūl*) – that I will certainly fill Hell with you and those that follow you – everyone" (38:84-85).

Comprising fifteen verses (38:71-85), the above Passage G contains many verses similar to those in each of the Passages B, C, D and E but it also differs from each of them in a number of verses. However, when we combine the latter four passages together we find that all the information in Passage G, except for several pieces, is already provided in these other passages. Two important pieces of information given in Passage G but not found in the other four passages are contained in verse 38:75. Both pieces pertain to God's creation of Ādam (peace be upon him!). God asked Iblīs why he failed to prostrate himself to Ādam (peace be upon him!) "whom I have created with My hands." The main message we get from this verse is that Ādam (peace be upon him!) was a special creation, and this revealed data provides a clear answer to the question of the origin of man. The other piece of information pertains to Satan's cosmic ontological status. When God asked Satan why he refused to prostrate himself to man into whom He has blown some Divine spirit He also suggested to him in the form of a question that the real reason for the refusal could only be one of two things. It was because he was either arrogant or one of the high ones (*min al-'ālīn*). However, God has made clear in the previous verse 38:74 that Satan was indeed haughty. So he could not be among the high ones, meaning man the microcosm whom God created with His hands and the angels.[253] Satan's claim to superiority over man on the ground that fire is superior to clay could only be a false or misplaced argument. The other piece of information in Passage G not found in exactly the same words as in the other four passages is contained in the verse 38:82, which pertains to the cosmic role of Satan. Upon being given respite by God till the Day of the Resurrection (38:80-81) after pleading to Him for it (38:79), Satan told Him, "Then, by Your power, I will put them all in the wrong except the sincere and the purified among Your servants" (38:82-83). This "oath of Satan" – to borrow Yusuf 'Ali's phrase[254] – is of profound importance to the understanding of the cosmic role of Satan within the scheme of God's creation of man. The two verses as a whole, and the phrase "by Your power (*'izza*)" in particular that Satan uses, points to his limited power in playing his role as man's number one enemy and, ultimately, even this limited power is derived from God's infinite power, all of which Satan himself acknowledges. From the point of view of our interest in

253. The verse 38:75 may be cited as a good proof of the inferiority of the subtle world of which Satan is a part to the angelic world in the hierarchy of beings in the cosmos.

254. 'Abdullah Yusuf 'Ali, *The Meaning of the Holy Qur'an*, p. 984, note 4234.

having a more detailed knowledge of man's microcosmic constitution, however, this Passage G does not add any substantial new information to the one already furnished by the Passages B, C, D, and E.

**The Idea of Microcosm in the Chapter of the Prostration (Passage F) and the Chapter of the Fig (Passage H)**

We now treat Passages F and H together with the view of deriving further information about the microcosmic constitution of man. Passage F reads:

> He Who has made everything which He has created most good: He began the creation of man with [nothing more than] clay (32:7),
>
> And made his progeny (*nasl*) from a quintessence of the nature of a fluid despised (32:8),
>
> But He fashioned and proportioned him, and breathed into him something of His Spirit. And He gave you [the faculties of] hearing and sight and feeling [and understanding]: little thanks do you give! (32:9)

Passage H reads as follows:

> We indeed created man in the best of constitution (95:4),
>
> Then We restore him to the lowest of the low (95:5)
>
> Except such as believe and do righteous deeds: for them shall be a reward unfailing (95:6)

These two passages do not refer to Ādam's creation but rather to that of his progeny, which is however modeled after his prototypal microcosmic constitution. Passage F provides new data about the biological and cognitive or noetic components of the microcosm not encountered in the previous passages. These data pertain to the physical elements of the human constitution that originate from clay (*ṭīn*) (32:7) and its non-physical elements that originate from the quintessential fluid (*sulālatin min mā'*) (32:8) as well as the various levels of man's cognitive powers or faculties. These cognitive powers allude to the partial Divine spirit in man, because they are its properties. All of these data would be of great help to our microcosmic interpretation of Passage H.

We interpret the Passage H as referring to man as a microcosm. The phrase "man in the best of constitution" (*al-insān fī aḥsan taqwīm*) in the verse 95:4 and the phrase "We restored him to the lowest of the low" (*radadnāhu asfala sāfilīn*) in the immediately following verse 95:5 point to the total dimensions of the microcosm. Passage F seems to support this interpretation. This passage seeks to assert the principle that "God made everything He has created most excellent (*aḥsan*)" (32:7) and it illustrates this principle with the example of the creation of man (*insān*) (32:7), the best example there is since man is created a microcosm. In describing man as having the most excellent form or constitution, the passage's verses 32:7-9 appeal to his proportioned body, soul, and spirit, including his physical, rational, and spiritual faculties as a clear evidence. Clay, sperm ("quintessential fluid"), proportioned body and soul, and the inblown Divine Spirit that are mentioned in the passage in that order together represent the totality of the qualitatively different dimensions of cosmic reality.

The word *taqwīm* conveys among others the meanings of

"mould, symmetry, form, nature, and constitution"[255] with each displaying many excellent properties and positive qualities.[256] In his translation of Ibn al-'Arabī's commentary on the verses 95:4-5 Chittick renders *aḥsan taqwīm* as "the most beautiful stature."[257] Ibn al-'Arabī interprets the verse "We indeed created man in the most beautiful stature" as being equivalent in meaning to God's words "Nothing is as His likeness (*laisa kamithlihi shay'*)"[258] and the Prophetic hadith "God created Ādam in His form."[259] Most exegetes, including Ibn 'Abbās,[260]

---

255. 'Abdullah Yusuf 'Ali, *The Meaning of the Holy Qur'an*, p. 1395, note 6199.

256. Asad renders *aḥsan taqwīm* as "the best conformation" the meaning of which he limits to the endowment of positive qualities, both physical and mental. See Muhammad Asad, *The Message of the Qur'an*, p. 1148, note 2. *Tafsīr ibn 'Abbās*, apparently in referring to the occasion of the revelation of the verse when Ibn 'Abbās (may God be pleased with him!) mentioned al-Walīd ibn al-Mughīrah and Kildah ibn Usayd as the either person to whom the phrase *aḥsan taqwīm* was attributed, interpreted it as "the best form." This *Tafsīr* remarks that the verses 95:4-5 together have been understood to have the following meaning: "We have created the children ofĀdam in the best of forms when they are in the pick of their youth, then We reduce them to abject old age whereby no good deed is recorded in their favor except that which they used to do in their youth and prime." See *Tafsīr ibn 'Abbās*, p. 763.

257. William C. Chittick, *The Self-Disclosure of God*, p. 305.

258. *The Qur'an*, chapter 42 ("The Consultation"), verse 11. The full verse reads: "[He is] the Creator (*fāṭir*) of the heavens and the earth: He has made for you pairs from among yourselves, and pairs among cattle: by this means does He multiply you: Nothing is as His likeness (*laisa kamithlihi shay'*), and He is the One that hears and sees [all things]."

259. See William C. Chittick, *The Self-Disclosure of God*, p. 305.

interpret the statement "Nothing is as His likeness" from the point of view of Divine Transcendence (*tanzīh*), but Ibn al-'Arabī interprets it from the perspectives of both transcendence and immanence (*tashbīh*). In conformity with the perspective of immanence Ibn al-'Arabī interprets "His likeness" as meaning "His form or image on the human plane, namely Ādam the Perfect Man (*al-insān al-kāmil*)." The statement "nothing is as His likeness" would then convey the idea of the perfection and uniqueness of the Adamic human configuration.

The phrase "the best of moulds and the most beautiful stature" (*aḥsan taqwīm*) also signifies the perfect form (*ṣūra*) of the Real (*al-ḥaqq*) in which God created the Adamic species. As for the following verse (95:5) "Then We restored (*radadnā*) him to the lowest of the low," Ibn al-'Arabī explains that it was with the view of "bringing together in Ādam (peace be upon him!) the perfection of the form of His Attributes and Qualities" that God brought him down to the "lowest of the low," because it was through their cosmological descent to the lowest of the low that each domain in the cosmological hierarchy displays their traces or signs, including the realm of the physical body.[261] On the basis of this explanation by Ibn al-'Arabī, we may assert that, in principle, the complete and perfect Adamic human constitution embraces elements from the whole cosmic hierarchical order. In other words, the verses 95:4-5 signify the idea of man (*al-insān*) as the microcosm.

From the point of view of our main interest in this chapter, namely to have a detailed understanding of the constituent parts of the human microcosm, we prefer in the context of the

---

260. *Tafsīr ibn 'Abbās*, p. 559.

261. William C. Chittick, *The Self-Disclosure of God*, p. 305.

verse to render *taqwīm* as "constitution" but without in any way disregarding the important participatory role of the ideas of mold, symmetry, form, and nature in the manifestation or realization of the constitution. We have seen their participatory role in the course of discussing the earlier passages. In fact, in our discussion of the Adamic reality in this chapter thus far, we have used the words "constitution" and "form" to convey meanings that are essentially interrelated. Depending on the context, each of these two entities could include the other. For example, when we are referring to the Adamic constitution as a whole, we would speak of it as comprising many forms, the most fundamental of which are the spiritual, the subtle, and the physical. However, when what is sought to be emphasized is the idea of the Adamic form – that is, God's own form in which He created Ādam (peace be upon him!) – as what Ibn al-'Arabī did in his interpretation of Passage H, then the Adamic form becomes a metaphysical basis and a determining principle of the Adamic constitution. In other words, Ādam's divine form determines his constitutional makeup.

We would go along with Ibn al-'Arabī's interpretation of passage G. In its light, we may speak of the Adamic constitution in more specific terms. We may understand the phrase "We restored him to the lowest of the low" as conveying the meaning that man in his most excellent constitution and form as indicated in the verse 95:4 is an hierarchical being, containing within himself various grades of being and levels of reality, stretching from the highest spiritual level to the lowest level, which is the physical. In terms of subjective experience or consciousness realization, open to man is the possibility of traversing the various levels of consciousness rooted in his soul. With respect to this subjective experience, the "lowest of the low" would be the psychological state of misery as symbolized by hell fire. When the verse 95:6 says that "the believers and the doers of righteous deeds" are exceptions to the general lot of mankind being dragged to the "lowest of the low," it means that their spiritual state is such that it is identifiable with the highest levels of consciousness. It is a worthy observation to make here that while Passage F presents the various levels of being and consciousness in the microcosmic reality in an ascending order of perfection toward the realization of the Perfect Man – symbolically from clay to the inblowing of the Divine Spirit – Passage H presents them in a descending order of imperfection toward damnation. This brief discussion of Passages F and H again shows that, like the earlier passages, they allude in a convincing manner to the reality of man as a microcosm.

## The Idea of the Microcosm in the Chapter of the Clinging Clot or "Read!" (Passage J)

Passage J, the last in our series of passages on the theme of the human microcosm, comprises the whole of chapter 96 ("The Clinging Clot" or "Read!). The passage reads as follows:

> Read! in the Name of your Lord and Cherisher, Who created – created man out of a [mere] clot of congealed blood (*'alaq*) (96:1-2).
>
> Read! and your Lord is the Most Bountiful One (*al-Akram*), Who taught [man] by means of the Pen (*al-qalam*) – taught man that which he knew not (96:3-5).
>
> Nay, but man does transgress all bounds, in that he looks upon himself as self-sufficient (96:6-7). Verily, to your Lord is the return [of all] (96:6-8).

> Do you see one who forbids a votary when he [turns] to pray? Do you see if he is [on the road] of guidance? Or enjoins righteousness? Do you see if he denies [Truth] and turns away? Doesn't he know that God does see? (96:9-14).
>
> Let him beware! If he desist not, We will drag him by the forelock – a lying sinful forelock! (96:15-16).
>
> Then, let him call [for help] to his council [of comrades]: We will call on the angels of punishment [to deal with him]! Nay, do not heed him, but bow down in adoration, and bring yourself the closer [to God] (96:17-19).

The above passage J deals in its entirety with the creation of man (*insān*) and his constitution. It alludes to the total constitution of man in the qualitative sense – physical, biological, psychological, intellectual-rational, and spiritual – although the physical and spiritual constituents or dimensions are not explicitly stated. Rather, the physical and spiritual elements are only implied. The physical constituent element is implied by the word *'alaq* ("clot of congealed blood"). *'Alaq* implies the sperm (*nuṭfah*) as verse 14, chapter 23 ("The Believers") states that God "made the sperm into a clot of congealed blood." And the sperm implies clay (*ṭīn*), since in the same chapter the two preceding verses (23:12-13) clearly mention that God created the sperm out of "a quintessence of clay" (*sulālatin min ṭīn*). This empirical, scientific fact in reproductive biology is also mentioned in our earlier Passage F, verse 32:7-8. Thus, in mentioning *'alaq* Passage J is in effect also referring to the quintessence of man's physical components.

Just as in Passage B, the Divine spirit that was blown into

man is not mentioned in the present passage J, but it is implied. It is implied by the word *al-qalam* ("the Pen"), the Divine instrument by means of which man gains knowledge of all kinds. Thanks to this "Pen" man becomes a sentient being. This "Pen" has been interpreted in several different ways without them necessarily contradicting each other. The interpretation we favor the most is the viewing and understanding of the Pen as alluding to man's intellect-reason (*'aql*). In the context of the history of man as a sentient being on earth, *al-qalam* could not be referring to the material pen of whatever it is made, since even before the invention of writing man has been making use of this "immaterial Pen." However, man's *'aql* with which he is endowed by God implies the manifestation of some Divine spirit in him. As we have maintained in another part of our discussion in this chapter, man's intellect-reason is the cognitive property of the Divine spirit that was blown into him. Thus the word *al-qalam* in passage H implies the presence of a spiritual dimension in man.

The biological component of man is indicated by the "clot of congealed blood" (*'alaq*). As mentioned by verse 23:14, it is out of this clot that God made "a [fetus] lump" (*mudghah*), then out of this lump "bones" (*'iẓām*) which he clothed with "flesh" (*laḥm*), and then out it a creature with human form. Thus *'alaq* implies both the non-living physical form of man, namely clay, and the various stages of animal forms that go into man's making. Passage H also mentions man's psychological structure as indicated by the two opposite kinds of tendencies and activities of the soul. The first kind refers to evil tendencies and activities of the soul as illustrated by its part that transgresses (96:6) bounds imposed by God and that likes to think of itself as self-sufficient and independent of God (96:7).

This part of the soul has also the capacity to forbid what is essentially and morally good for man such as prayer (96:9-10), oppose Divine guidance and righteousness (96:11-12), and deny the Truth (96:13). The second kind of the soul's tendencies is indicated by its capacity not to heed evil, to prostrate oneself before God, and to be drawn close to Him (96:19). These higher tendencies of man of which he is frequently reminded by God allude to the presence of a spiritual dimension in his constitution. Viewing together all these various constituents of man, we may assert that Passage J is indeed referring to his microcosmic constitution.

**The Chronological Order of Revelation on the Idea of Microcosm: Its Significance for the Muslim Mind**

In this section, we intend to look closely at the chronological order of revelation of all the microcosm passages except of the Opening Chapter – B, C, D, E, F, G, H and J – that we have discussed to see if we can attach any significance to it. It appears that while the lettering of these passages is in the increasing order of their appearance in the numbered chapters of the Qur'an,[262] their chronological order of revelation is exactly the opposite. Passage J (96:1-19) was the earliest to be revealed. In fact, as every Muslim knows, the first five verses of this passage constitute the Prophet's maiden revelation, which he was said to have received in Mecca in the last third of the

262. There is, however, one lettering sequence which does not accord with the ascending numerical order of the chapters. Passage E belongs to chapter 38, while passage F belongs to chapter 32.

month of Ramadan, thirteen years before the Hijra.[263] It is extremely significant that the first revelation addresses the issue of the creation of the whole man (*insān*) and his constitution, a theme to be later taken up in our list of passages from varying perspectives. The central and constant element in this theme is the idea of man as the microcosm, although it is not explicitly mentioned. The constituents of man explicitly stated and implied in the maiden revelation are complemented in a complete way by other data on his constituents that are provided by the rest of Passage J (verses 6-19)[264] and the other listed passages as our previous discussions have clearly shown.

According to the Qur'an, the central aim of God's revelation is to provide knowledge to man of who he really is in relation to his Creator. It is therefore only fitting that the first revelation states some of the fundamental facts about man's nature that would help to restore his lost dignity. Although of a lowly origin, man has been conferred dignity by God on account of his being created as a sentient being. The Prophet's early followers understood well this Divine message. The revelation needed to be proclaimed to men, but it invited opposition. Given this opposition, an explanation of another

---

263. According to calculations, the attributed time of the Prophet's maiden revelation would correspond to July or August 610 A.D. of the Christian era.

264. According to almost all the authorities, the Prophet's second revelation did not come until after a lapse or what is popularly referred to as *fatrah* ("interval or break") of some months or perhaps even over a year. The second revelation by the way is not the rest of Passage J but a considerable part of chapter 68 significantly titled "The Pen," since it begins with God swearing by the symbolic Pen mentioned in the first revelation. However, verses 6-19 of Passage J were considered to be revealed not long after the *fatrah*.

side of man – the capacity for evil – that runs counter to his dignity as a sentient being was called for. The second part of Passage J with the exception of verse 96:19 provides the psychological basis for the understanding of man's opposition to the Divine call and his evil doings and their consequences in the form of Divine punishment. Verse 96:19 affirms the way of life that God preferred men to lead, namely a spiritual life of close proximity to Him. It provides the psychological basis for man's spiritual capacity, which in reality is far more fundamental and greater than his evil capacity. In the light of this emerging feud between the forces of good and the forces of evil in Mecca, it is most appropriate that verses 96:6-19 were combined with the maiden revelation to constitute a coherent single chapter.

As for Passage H (95:4-6) and the whole chapter to which it belongs, it was revealed during the early Meccan period of the Prophet's mission. It was the second earliest of verses in the Qur'an to be revealed dealing with the theme of the human constitution. It describes the whole of the human configuration in the most essential terms that transcend particularistic manifestations along such lines as gender, ethnic differentiation, skin color, and mother tongue. It describes man (*al-insān*) as being created in "the best of moulds and the most beautiful stature" (*aḥsan taqwīm*). The hierarchic range of the qualitative elemental content of the Adamic configuration is best described in this passage. There is continuity between Passages H and J in affirming a universal conception of man based on his true nature that is attributed to the whole of the human species. This continuity is only to be expected of the new revelation, which seeks to establish the identity of Islam as a universal religion on the solid foundation of a comprehensive conception of man with his unique nature and constitution. The early Muslim minds see in this Passage H a further elaboration and clarification as well as confirmation of the truths about man revealed in Passage J.

Passage G (38:71-85) was the third earliest of such a set of verses to be revealed, also during the earlier part of the Meccan period but toward the middle part of it.[265] This passage tells us that the complete man is constituted of *bashar* made from clay (*ṭīn*) and something of the Divine Spirit blown into it. Man as created by God is partly of lowly origin, namely clay from which *bashar* is made, and partly of Divine origin by virtue of which the angels bowed down to him. In the eyes of Iblīs, man is just his *bashar* and for that presumed reason he refused to prostrate himself to him. The distinguished personalities of Mecca, who rejected and opposed the Prophet (salutation and peace be upon him!) and his message, did so primarily on the argument that he was an ordinary man understood as *bashar*,[266] just like any other man, and he could not therefore be a recipient of revelation from God. The word *bashar* perhaps

265. According to Asad, it was probably revealed "toward the end of the fourth or the beginning of the fifth year of the Prophet's mission." Muhammad Asad, *The Message of the Qur'an*, p. 829. Yusuf 'Ali describes the passage E and the chapter to which it belongs as being revealed in the early middle Meccan period. Abdullah Yusuf 'Ali, *The Meaning of the Holy Qur'an*, p. 948 and p. 970.

266. The earliest occurrence of the word *bashar* in the Qur'an is said to be attributed to Walīd ibn al-Mughayrah, a wealthy Sybarite, and Abū Jahl, both staunch enemies of the Prophet (salutation and peace be upon him!). The Qur'an, chapter 74 ("The One Wrapped Up"), verses 24-25, says: "Then said he: "This is nothing but magic, derived from of old; this is nothing but the word of a *bashar* ("mortal")!""

entered the vocabulary of the Qur'an for the first time through chapter 74[267] ("The One Wrapped Up"), which is considered by many authorities to be the Prophet's fourth revelation.[268]

We have earlier touched very briefly on the meaning of this word as it occurred in Passages D and E. Given the great significance of the idea of *bashar* to God's creation of *insān*, to Iblīs' refusal to bow down to Ādam (peace be upon him!), and to the disbelievers' rejection of the idea of human recipients of Divine messages, there is a need to explain the precise meaning of *bashar* as used in the Qur'an generally and in passages D and F in particular. The word *bashar* is mentioned thirty-seven times in the Qur'an. The noun *bashar*[269] is derived from the root verb *bashara* that conveys the core meaning of "to remove the face or surface of a thing or the skin of the body upon which the hair grew from its flesh."[270] The root verb also means "to expose to view the exterior of a body" and this exterior includes complexion (*basharat*). The whole semantic field of the root verb *bashara* that includes its application to bodies other than the human body such as even the earth[271] points

267. The word *bashar* occurs four times in this chapter, namely in verses 74:25; 74:29; 74:31; 74:36.

268. 'Abdullah Yusuf 'Ali, *The Meaning of the Holy Qur'an*, p. 1294. The third revelation is said to be chapter 73 ("The Enfolded One"), and the second part of Passage J (96:6-19) came after chapter 74.

269. Classical lexicologists maintained that the words *bashar* and *basharat* are synonymous. See Edward W. Lane, *Arabic-English Lexicon*, vol. 1, p. 208.

270. Edward W. Lane, *Arabic-English Lexicon*, vol. 1, p. 207.

271. Thus we have the statement *bashara al-arḍ* to convey the meaning of a swarm of locusts "stripping the ground" or "eating what was upon the

clearly to its core idea of the externalities of a body.

As applied to the human being, the word *bashar* in classical Arabic usage signifies both male and female. It is used alike as singular and plural and dual. It is also used to signify the whole mankind (*al-bashar*).[272] Thus we find Ādam (peace be upon him!) being referred to as *abū'l-bashar* ("the father of mankind").[273]This unique linguistic feature pertaining to the usage of the word *bashar* may be interpreted as an affirmation of the exterior aspect of the Adamic constitution that is common to all human beings regardless of their gender and plurality. When we examine carefully the qur'anic usage of the word *bashar*, we find that the Qur'an has broadened the semantics of the word beyond what was understood in the pre-Islamic Arabic. In accordance with the original linguistic meaning of the word *bashar*, the Qur'an uses it to signify the exterior part of the Adamic human constitution in contradistinction to its interior part. As pointed out by Ibn al-'Arabī, *bashar* refers to man's "natural constitution" that is made up of compounded elements, as distinct from its supra-natural or spiritual dimension of the Adamic constitution. In classical Islamic scientific thought, man's natural constitution is understood to comprise elements from the corporeal and subtle worlds that are proportioned and balanced in such a way that it is in a state of preparedness to serve as a receptacle of

---

ground or its surface" as if the surface of the earth is its *basharat* or *bashar*. Edward W. Lane, *Arabic-English Lexicon*, vol. 1, p. 207,

272. In some of its verses, the Qur'an also appears to be using the word *bashar* in the sense of mankind. See chapter 74 ("The One Wrapped Up"), verse 31 and verse 36.

273. Edward W. Lane, *Arabic-English Lexicon*, vol. 1, p. 208.

some of the Divine Spirit that is blown into it.

In the terminology employed in their characteristically Peripatetic faculty psychology, classical Muslim philosopher-scientists referred to man's *bashar* as composed of elements of the three kingdoms in the natural world, namely the mineral, the plant, and the animal kingdoms. Since one of their guiding principles is that every living entity possesses a soul, plants and animals are presented as having souls. Further, souls are the governing principles of bodies with which they are respectively associated and connected. A soul is understood as having powers (sing: *qūwah*). Souls are ranked according to the powers they each have. Because of their greater complexity in terms of elemental composition and functions, animal souls are understood as having more powers than plant souls. Elements of the natural world as understood by these philosopher-scientists are not quantitative in nature as what we have in modern chemistry but rather qualitative as maintained in traditional Islamic science and, in fact, in all pre-modern sciences of the world.

The theories of elements in Islamic science and modern science are based on two different ways of looking at the divisions of the physical or material world. In its past history, Islamic science adopted in the main a qualitative division of the physical world. To be sure, an "atomic division" of matter into smaller and smaller particles that is akin to the modern atomic theory but, unlike it, not totally quantitative was found in Islamic thought associated with certain schools of *kalām* ("dialectical theology") and Sufism. Qualitative and quantitative theories of the elements that are at the basis of the physical world are not necessarily opposed to each other. They both have strengths and limitations in their applicability in science. Islamic civilization has clearly shown that it is possible to create a science based on a qualitative theory of elements, by which we mean the traditional theory of the four elements, namely earth, water, air, and fire. Modern science too has shown that it is possible to create a science on the basis of a quantitative theory of elements, the known number of which is 118. In our view, just as in many other areas of scientific knowledge, a synthesis of the two theories of elements is called for in our contemporary human civilization. The worthiness of each theory dictates this synthesis.

In describing the elemental composition of man's physical body, which is the exterior part of his *bashar*, the Qur'an uses the theory of the four elements. We will discuss in greater details in the last section of this chapter the meaning and significance of *bashar* as God's creation from the scientific point of view. Chronologically, the significance of Passage G in relation to the earlier passages, including Passages J and H,[274] lies in the fact that opposition to the Prophet's mission from the Chiefs of the disbelievers in Mecca had entered a new phase in which they sought to justify their opposition by appealing to their reductionistic conception of man. In their view, man including the Prophet was just his *bashar*.[275] Passage G was

274. Chronologically, Passage G was preceded by passages J and H, the greater part of chapter 68 ("The Pen"), and chapters 73 ("The Enfolded One") and 74 ("The One Wrapped Up"). Prior to Passage G, chapter 74 has already made references to *bashar* one instance of which is its quotation of the usage of the word by Walīd ibn al-Mughayrah. See note 81.

275. See chapter 74, verse 25 for the view of Walīd ibn al-Mughayrah, a staunch Pagan and wealthy dignitary of Mecca, who was a bitter foe of the Prophet (salutation and peace be upon him!) and his mission.

meant to show that their view was false, but it wanted to demonstrate it in terms of arguments that are generally applicable to all such situations at other times and in different places. There will always be people in the future and somewhere on earth, who subscribe to this erroneous view of man. The way Passage G has responded to the "*bashar* argument" is to explain that it has its origin in the prototypal argument of Iblīs, who cited the same reason for refusing to bow down to man after some Divine spirit is already blown into him. Moreover, although the word *bashar* was mentioned earlier in chapter 74, Passage G paraded itself as the first instance in which God presented the idea within the framework of man's constitution as a microcosm.

Passage F (32:7-9) is the fourth of the lettered eight passages on the microcosm to be revealed to the Prophet (salutation and peace be upon him!). According to Yusuf 'Ali, it belongs to the middle Meccan period,[276] while Asad thinks that it was revealed during the late Meccan period.[277] Either view would confirm the chronological position of Passage F as being revealed later than Passage G. The whole Passage F is about the reproduction of man as a microcosm, and as such it is loaded with issues of scientific concern to both Islamic and modern sciences. It may be seen as an elaboration and a detailing of the microcosmic constitution of man alluded to in its preceding passages, particularly of the biological entity *'alaq* mentioned

---

276. 'Abdullah Yusuf 'Ali, *The Meaning of the Holy Qur'an*, p. 868.

277. Muhammad Asad, *The Message of the Qur'an*, p. 755. Asad brought attention to the view held by some commentators that verses 16-20 of the chapter, which anyway do not belong to our passage under discussion, were revealed in Medina. He, however, dismissed the claim as purely speculative.

in the maiden revelation.

Passage E (20:115-124) is generally accepted by the commentators of the Qur'an to have been revealed as early as the seventh year before the Hijrah, which means to say that just before the middle of the Meccan period.[278] A portion of the chapter to which this passage belongs is historically linked to 'Umar ibn al-Khaṭṭāb's conversion to Islam,[279] which took place about that year. The various views held by the commentators concerning the respective times of revelation of Passages F and E seem to indicate that the latter passage is preferable to the former passage to be considered as the earlier of the two to be revealed, although the two revelations could have occurred within a very short period of time. The thrust of Passage E is on the spiritual and psychological dimensions of Ādam's microcosmic constitution, which by extension are also those of his progeny. A part of this Adamic constitution – the lower soul that is prone to evil (*al-nafs la-ammārah*) (12:53) – is

---

278. Both Yusuf 'Ali and Asad concur on the chronological position of passage D. See 'Abdullah Yusuf 'Ali, *The Meaning of the Holy Qur'an*, p. 630 (introduction to chapter 20); Muhammad Asad, *The Message of the Qur'an*, p. 561.

279. According to well-known traditional sources, 'Umar ibn al-Khaṭṭāb (may God be pleased with him!), a close companion of the Prophet (salutation and peace be upon him!) who became the second Caliph of Islam after his death, converted to Islam after reading a written copy of some portion of chapter *Ṭā Ḥā* which he had forced his sister Fāṭimah and her husband Sa'ad to hand over to him. This dramatic confrontation between brother and sister occurred at her house after 'Umar ibn al-Khaṭṭāb (may God be pleased with him!) became furious at learning that she and her husband had converted to Islam. As destiny has it, 'Umar's soul was deeply touched by what he read, and he decided to convert to Islam as well.

susceptible to attacks and manipulations by Satan, a symbol of prototypal evil, whom God declares is man's number one enemy. The main purpose of this thrust of the passage is to convey God's warning to man to always be alert and vigilant of Satan's evil doings such as temptations and allurements and to preempt them with safeguards in the form of obedience to God's guidance.

The concluding verse of Passage E (20:124) is to serve as a reminder to every human being on the dire consequences of rejecting God's message. The content of this Passage and its textual contexts – its preceding as well as succeeding verses[280] – seem to be alluding to the social context of its revelation, namely an intensification of the conflict and confrontation between the followers and the oppositionists of the new religion. It is in the nature of the Qur'an's depiction of any human conflict of deep significance to cast it in spiritual terms so that man may derive broader lessons from it. The reference in the passage to Ādam's encounter with the deceitful Satan as the embodiment of evil, who brought about his spiritual fall, and his return to the straight path thanks to Divine mercy and guidance serves the purpose of providing the necessary spiritual perspectives on the conflict in Mecca.

Passage D (15:26-42) is regarded by most commentators as

---

280. Verses preceding Passage E refer to the spiritual fall of Pharaoh and the Samiri, the former through arrogance and the other through mischief and false harking back to tradition. Its succeeding verses refer to God's punishment of the transgressors and the disbelievers in His signs both in the present life and in the hereafter. Clearly, these references equally apply to the Chieftains in Mecca who persecuted the Prophet (salutation and peace be upon him!) and his followers.

being revealed during the latter part of the Meccan period.[281] The main thrust of this passage is God's message concerning man's microcosmic constitution that makes him God's best creation. This "cosmic fact" invites acknowledgment from the angels expressed through their obeisance to God's command but only jealousy and arrogance from Iblīs that makes him rebel against Him. The main purpose of this thrust is to impress upon man that in his inevitable encounter with evil[282] in his earthly sojourn good will triumph over evil, since his constitutional makeup has been structured in such a way that his innate capacity for good and guidance far outstrips that for evil. If man is sincere in his willing to live a divinely guided life, then evil would be powerless to prevail over him. Revealed at a time when persecution of the Prophet (salutation and peace be upon him!) and his followers was at its worst, the content of the passage is most understandable. It was to give spiritual comfort to the believers and instill in them determination and fortitude

281. Suyuṭī maintains the view that the chapter to which this passage belongs was revealed very shortly after chapter 12 ("Yūsuf"), implying that its revelation took place during the last year before the Prophet's Hijra. See Muhammad Asad, *The Message of the Qur'an*, p. 457. Yusuf 'Ali also puts its time of revelation in the second half of the Meccan period, but favors pushing it back closer to the middle of that period. See 'Abdullah Yusuf 'Ali, *The Meaning of the Holy Qur'an*, p. 507. In the light of all the views expressed, the certainty is that Passage D is chronologically later than Passages H, G, F and E.

282. Cosmologically speaking, man's "inevitable encounter with evil" arises from the fact that Iblīs or Satan has a cosmic role to play as his greatest enemy in God's scheme of creation as clearly implied by His granting of respite to him until the end of the world. Satan takes full advantage of this respite to assault every human being from all sides.

in their war against the forces of evil and confidence that paradise would be their reward from God and hell the abode for the disbelievers. The theme of Divine providence in this world in the verses preceding Passage D and of Divine providence in the next life in the verses succeeding it provides the appropriate textual context for the passage.

The chapter to which Passage C (7:10-25) belongs, according to most of the commentators, including Ibn 'Abbās (may God be pleased with him!), was revealed during the last year before the Prophet's Hijra. The main thrust of this passage is on several key issues, namely man's cosmic status as the best creation, the acknowledgment of this status by the angels, Iblīs' jealousy, arrogance and rebellion, Satan's vow to use the respite period granted by God to assault human beings from all sides, the spiritual fall of Ādam (peace be upon him!) and Eve through deceit, Ādam's acknowledgment to God of his own sin and his sincere desire to return to the straight path and the spiritual prerequisites that the return entails, and God's designation of the planet Earth as man's temporary home. Like Passage D, Passage C that was revealed "on the eve of the Hijra" contains many ideas and issues that were pertinent to the state of the Muslim mind at the time. Passage C was similarly meant to provide the cosmic and spiritual contexts for the conflict between the believers and the disbelievers. The specific revelation of which Passage C is a part was aimed at removing the immense psychological burden on the Prophet as a result of the great difficulty he was facing and providing spiritual lessons to the believers to strengthen their faith and warning the disbelievers of their dire punishment (7:2). The common theme of the verses preceding Passage C and those succeeding it is about the conflict between those who accept the Divine message and those who reject it and its final outcome.

Passage B (2:30-39) belongs to the longest chapter of the Qur'an that was entirely revealed in Medina. The main thrust of the passage is on the creation of Ādam (peace be upon him!) as God's vicegerent (*khalīfah*) who is to be placed on the planet Earth, the necessary qualifications for this specially created job, the main duties and responsibilities dictated by the job, its major challenges and obstacles, and the need for Divine guidance in man's earthly life. The creation of Ādam (peace be upon him!) as a microcosm appears to be the most fundamental condition and qualification for the purpose of assuming the role and function of God's *khalīfah*. This hereditary role and function which is inherited by every one of his progeny implies that every human being is created with a microcosmic constitution.

In the light of our discussion thus far of the idea of man as a microcosm, it is possible to argue that this idea is a key conceptual component of the Qur'anic worldview. Unfortunately, this fact is seldom mentioned in contemporary discussions of the Islamic worldview that occupy so many Muslim minds. Perhaps, the main reason for this unfortunate intellectual situation is simply the lack of an awareness of the importance of the idea to a proper and true understanding of the concept of creation of man according to the Qur'an. Or, the idea of the human microcosm is just not well understood by many people. Yet in our view, this idea presents itself as one of the most fundamental concepts in the formulation of the Islamic worldview.

We may further argue that the best proofs of the core position of this idea in the Qur'anic worldview are provided by both the chronological and the textual contexts of the main passages in which the idea is embedded that we have discussed. If these passages are studied in a chronological sequence, as we have just done, albeit only briefly, then we can discern an inner logic that justifies the sequence. It was as if God wanted to educate the Prophet's followers on the true conception of man in a logical fashion and in a very practical way as required by the chronological context of each of the revealed passages with the view of having a maximum pedagogical impact on their minds. From a certain point of view, we may take note of the fact that except for Passage B, all the Passages we have discussed were revealed in Mecca before the foundation of the first Muslim community (*umma*) and the first Muslim state in Medina under the leadership of the Prophet (salutation and peace be upon him!).

This fact goes to show the importance of the idea of human microcosm to the shaping of the Muslim mind. We have made reference in this chapter to ʿAlī ibn Abī Ṭālib (may God be pleased with him!) as the coiner of the Arabic term for microcosm, namely *al-ʿālam al-ṣaghīr*, to emphasize the early currency of this idea in an explicit manner in traditional Islamic thought. In this connection, we are also quite familiar with the view held by some Muslims that there is a good basis for regarding the two periods of the Prophetic era providentially separated by the Hijra as having distinct characteristics and features in a number of respects. The most widely discussed aspect of this view pertains to the dimensions and domains of the religion that were given emphasis and focus in each period. It is claimed that the focus of the Meccan revelations was on the exposition of who God is, what His creation is, who man is, and man's final return to God. In other words, the focus was theology, metaphysics, cosmology, spiritual anthropology and psychology, and eschatology. On the basis of our discussion of man as the microcosm, it is quite clear that this idea falls within the concern of cosmology and spiritual anthropology and psychology.

It is further claimed that the focus in question has in view the structuring and the shaping of the individual Muslim mind in accordance with the new belief system as well as the shaping of his spiritual attitudes and virtues modeled after the Prophet's exemplary personality. In Mecca, the priority was said to be on the spiritual, intellectual, and moral development of the individual, while in Medina it was on the organization and development of the community on the basis of more detailed moral and ethical-legal principles, rules, and regulations. The Meccan period is presented as being a necessary preparatory ground for the realization of a moral communal life in all domains of society. We would go along with this way of distinguishing between the Meccan and Medinan periods provided that we do not push it too far to the point of implying that there is a complete break or discontinuity between the two periods or that they are mutually exclusive in terms of issues raised and emphasis laid.

There is continuity between them in emphasis on the supremacy of the same spiritual values and perspectives of things. However, the domains, the scopes or the detailing of their applications are not the same in the two periods for the simple and obvious reason that, in Medina, the spiritual understanding and virtues acquired in Mecca were applied to the whole realm of societal and communitarian concerns. The Meccan revelations too were concerned with such fundamental societal issues as illiteracy and the mistreatment of women, orphans, and the poor. However, while these revelations laid down the spiritual and moral foundation of Islam's social teachings and helped to produce men and women imbued with these teachings, the then dominant socio-political culture of Mecca did not permit them to be put into practice in the wider societal setting. The social philosophy of the new religion actually stood in opposition against this dominant Meccan culture.

The Prophet's Hijra with his best followers to the city of Yathrib, which he renamed Medina, was historic in more ways than one. It marked the birth of a new era in which Islam became the religion of a community and a state. Islam thus became a social reality and a civilization in the making. Those interested in establishing whether or not there was a significant difference in emphasis and orientation between the revelations in Mecca and the ones in Medina may wish to examine closely the specific case of the eight passages on the idea of the human microcosm. Each one of the passages revealed in Mecca emphasizes different aspects of man's microcosmic constitution. However, all of them seek to impress upon the Muslim mind the centrality of man in God's creation and his superiority to all other creatures.

# Bibliography


Asad, Muhammad (transl., explan.), *The Message of the Qur'an* (Gibraltar: Dar Al-Andalus, 1980).

Ayoub, Mahmoud M., *The Qur'an and Its Interpreters* (Albany: State University of New York Press, 1994), 2 volumes; reprint (Kuala Lumpur: Islamic Book Trust, 2012).

Bakar, Osman, *Classification of Knowledge in Islam* (Kuala Lumpur: Institute for Policy Studies, 1992); reprinted (Cambridge, UK: The Islamic Texts Society, 1998); reprinted (Lahore: Suhayl Academy, 1998); reprinted (Kuala Lumpur: ISTAC, IIUM, 2006).

____, *Tawhid and Science: Essays in History and Philosophy of Islamic Science* (Kuala Lumpur-Penang: Nurin Enterprise & Universiti Sains Malaysia, 1991).

____, *Tawhid and Science: Islamic Perspectives on Religion and Science* (Shah Alam, Malaysia: ARAH Publications, 2008).

____, *The History and Philosophy of Islamic Science* (Cambridge: Islamic Texts Society, 1997).

____, 'Cosmology,' Esposito, John L., ed., *The Oxford Encyclopedia of the Modern Islamic World* (New York-Oxford: Oxford University Press, 1995), vol. 1, pp. 322-328.

____, *Environmental Wisdom for Planet Earth: The Islamic Heritage* (Kuala Lumpur: University of Malaya Press, 2007).

____, 'Cosmology and models of the cosmos,' Kalin, Ibrahim, ed., *The*

*Oxford Encyclopedia of Philosophy, Science and Technology in Islam* (Oxford University Press,), vol. pp. 156 – 163.

Bett, Henry, *Johannes Scotus Erigena: A Study in Medieval Philosophy* (Cambridge: Cambridge University Press, 1925; reprinted 1964).

Bucaille, Maurice, *The Bible, The Quran and Science*, trans. (from French) Pannell, Alastair D. and author (Tripoli, Libya: Islamic Call Society, 1976); numerous reprints, including (Indianapolis: North American Trust Publications, 1978).

Burckhardt, Titus, *Alchemy, Science of the Cosmos, Science of the Soul*, trans. (from German), Stoddart, William (London: Stuart and Watkins, 1967); numerous reprints, the latest (Louisville, Kentucky: Fons Vitae, 2001).

Chittick, William C., *The Self-Disclosure of God: Principles of Ibn al-'Arabi's Cosmology* (Albany: State University of New York, 1998).

____, *The Sufi Path of Knowledge: Ibn al-'Arabi's Metaphysics of Imagination* (Albany: State University of New York, 1989).

____, *Science of the Cosmos, Science of the Soul: The Pertinence of Islamic Cosmology in the Modern World* (Oxford: One world Publications, 2007)

Corbin, Henry, *Avicenna and the Visionary Recital*, trans. from French, Willard R. Trask (Irving, Texas: Spring Publications, 1980).

Fakhry, Majid, *A History of Islamic Philosophy* (New York-London: Columbia University, 1983).

Fayrūzābādī, Abū Ṭāhir Muḥammad b. Ya'qūb al-, *Tanwīr al-Maqbās min Tafsīr Ibn 'Abbās* (Cairo: Al-Halabi and Sons, 1370 AH/1951 CE). Translated into English by Mokrane Guezzou (Ammanb: Royal Aal al-Bayt Institute for Islamic Thought, 2008); and (Louisville, Kentucky: Fons Vitae, 2008).

Al-Ghazzālī, *The Ninety-Nine Beautiful Names of God* ("*Al-maqṣad al-asnā fī sharḥ asmā' Allāh al-ḥusnā*"), trans. with notes, David B. Burrell and Nazih Daher (Cambridge, UK: The Islamic Texts Society, 1992).

____, *Mishkāt al-anwār* ("The Niche of Lights"), W. H. T. Gairdner, trans. (Lahore: Sh. Muhammad Ashraf, 1952).

Haq, Syed Nomanul, *Names, Natures and Things: The Alchemist Jabir Ibn Hayyan and His Kitāb al-Ahjār* (Boston: 1994).

Heinen, Anton, *Islamic Cosmology* (Beirut: Orient Institute, 1982).

Ikhwān al-Ṣafā', *Dispute between Man and the Animals,* trans. J. Platts (London: W. H. Allen, 1869).

____, *The Case of the Animals versus Man Before the King of the Jinn,* trans. Lenn Evan Goodman (Boston: Twayne Publishers, 1978).

Iqbal, Muzaffar, *Islam and Science* (Aldershot UK: Ashgate, 2002).

Izutsu, Toshihiko, *God and Man in the Qur'an: Semantics of the Qur'anic Weltanschaung* (Tokyo: Keio University, 1964); also (Kuala Lumpur: Islamic Book Trust, 2002 edition).

Khalid, Fazlun and Joanne O'Brien (eds.), *Islam and Ecology* (London: World Wide Fund for Nature, 1992).

King, David, *Astronomy in the Service of Islam* (Aldershot: Variorum, 1993).

____, *Islamic Mathematical Astronomy* (London: Variorum, 1986).

Lane, E. W., *Arabic-English Lexicon* (Cambridge: The Islamic Texts Society, 1984 edition), 2 vols.

Murata, Sachiko and William Chittick, *The Vision of Islam* (New York: Paragon House, 1994).

El-Naggar, Zaghloul R. M., *Tafsīr al-āyāt al-kawniyyah fi'l-Qur'ān al-Karīm* ("Exegesis on Verses on the Cosmic Phenomena in the Noble Qur'an") (Cairo: Maktabat al-Shuruq al-Dawliyyah, 2007-2008), 4 vols.

Nasr, Seyyed Hossein, *An Introduction to Islamic Cosmological Doctrines* (Cambridge, MA: Harvard University Press, 1964) and (London: Thames & Hudson, 1978).

____, *Islamic Science: An Illustrated Study* (London: World of Islam Festival Publishing Co. Ltd., 1976, repr. Chicago: Kazi Publications, 1995).

____, *Man and Nature: The Spiritual Crisis of Modern Man* (London: HarperCollins, 1989).

____, *Knowledge and the Sacred* (New York: Crossroad, 1981).

____, *Science and Civilization in Islam* (Cambridge MA: Harvard University Press, 1968, repr. London: Islamic Texts Society, 2003).

____, *Sufi Essays* (Albany: State University of New York Press, 1973).

____, *The Encounter of Man and Nature* (London: Allen and Unwin, 1968, repr. as *Man and Nature*, Chicago: ABC International, 1997).

____, 'The cosmos and the natural order,' Nasr, S. H., ed., *Islamic Spirituality: Foundations*, vol. 19 of World Spirituality: An Encyclopedic History of the Religious Quest (New York: Crossroad, 1987), pp. 345 – 357.

____, *Religion and the Order of Nature: The 1994 Cadbury Lectures at the University of Birmingham* (New York-Oxford: Oxford University Press, 1996).

____, 'The question of cosmogenesis – the cosmos as a subject of scientific study,' *Islam & Science*, 4 (2006), pp. 43-60.

Peters, Ted; Iqbal, Muzaffar; and Haq, Syed Nomanul, eds., *God, Life and the Cosmos: Christian and Muslim Perspectives* (Aldershot: Ashgate, 2002).

Al-Raghīb, Abū'l-Qāsim Ḥusayn, *Al-Mufradāt fī Gharīb al-Qur'ān* (Lebanon: Dar al-Ma'rifah, 2001).

Rahman, Fazlur, *Major Themes of the Qur'an* (Minnneapolis: Bibliotheca Islamica, 1994; 2nd edition).

Al-Rāzī, Fakhr al-Dīn, *Al-Tafsīr al-kabīr* ("The Great Commentary") or *Mafātiḥ al-ghayb* ("Keys to the Unseen") (Beirut: Dar al-Fikr, 1981).

Rahman, Fazlur, *Major Themes of the Qur'an* (Minnneapolis: Bibliotheca Islamica, 1994; 2nd edition).

Saliba, George, *A History of Arabic Astronomy: Planetary Theories during the Golden Age of Islam* (New York: New York University Press, 1994).

____, *Islamic Science and the Making of the European Renaissance* (Cambridge MA: MIT Press, 2007).

Schuon, Fritjof, *Dimensions of Islam* (London: Allen & Unwin, 1970).

Smith, Wolfgang, *Cosmos and Transcendence: Breaking through the Barrier of Scientistic Belief* (Peru, Illinois: Sherwood Sugden, 1984).

Al-Sulāmī, Abū ʻAbd al-Raḥmān, *The Subtleties of the Ascension: Early Mystical Sayings on Muhammad's Heavenly Journey* (Louisville, Kentucky: Fons Vitae, 2006).

Suyūṭī, Jalāl al-Dīn and Heinan, Anton M., *Islamic Cosmology: A Study of as-Suyūṭī's al-hay'a as-sanīya fi'l-hay'a as-sunnīya* (Wiesbaden: Steiner, 1982).

Al-Ṭabāṭabā'ī, Sayyid Muḥammad Ḥusayn, *Al-Mīzān fī tafsīr al-Qur'ān* (Beirut: Mu'assasat al-a'lami li'l-matbu'at, 1393-1394/1973-1974).

The Supreme Council for Islamic Affairs, ed., *Al-Muntakhab fī tafsīr al-Qur'ān al-karīm* (Cairo, 1973).

Yusuf ʻAli, ʻAbdullah, *The Meaning of the Holy Qur'an: Text, Translation and Commentary* (Kuala Lumpur: Islamic Book Trust, 2009).

# Index

Printed in the USA
CPSIA information can be obtained
at www.ICGtesting.com
LVHW090430211223
767012LV00003B/250

9 789670 526256